Close Your Eyes & Open Your Mind

An introduction to spiritual meditation

Dada Nabhaniilananda

Close Your Eyes & Open Your Mind

An introduction to spiritual meditation

Dada Nabhaniilananda

InnerWorld Publications

Published by:

InnerWorld Publications
P.O. Box 1455
Waitsfield VT 05673
USA

Distributed by Eternalwave: www.eternalwave.com

ISBN 1-881717-07-0

Book design by Devanistha/Jody Wright
Front cover photo: Krsna Deva
Back cover photo: Hitendra
Photos inside by Ramakrsna, Satya, Dada Nabhaniilananda

Printed in the United States of America.

10 9 8 7 6 5 4 3 2 1

Dedication

To an old friend,
without whom this book
would never have been written.

Acknowledgements

Firstly I would like to thank all my meditation students who over the years, have inspired me with their sincerity and with their insightful questions and have helped me to understand how to teach this subject more effectively. Many others have helped with this book, and I cannot mention them all, but of particular note are Jayanta Kumar, Malati, Devashiish, Dada Jyotirupananda, Geoff Hooper, Krsna Deva, Phanendra, Manorainjan, Dada Giridevananda, Dada Maheshvarananda, Amal, Jyotirmaya, John Hills, Giridhara, Devanistha and Dada Gunamuktananda. I'd also like to thank my Acarya who first taught me meditation, and more than anyone, my Guru Shrii Shrii Anandamurti.

Table of Contents

Introduction..vii

Chapter 1: Start with Questions................................2

What is meditation?..2
What is self-realisation?..3
What is the difference between meditation and yoga?.........3
What is the difference between prayer and meditation?........4
Is meditation a science?..5
What is spirituality?...5
Is spirituality scientific?...6
What is mysticism?..7
What is the difference between spirituality and religion?......7
What is spiritual meditation?..9
Do you have to be a monk to be successful in meditation?...9
Isn't it self-centred to sit around meditating all the time when
    there is so much suffering in the world?..........................10
Is meditation a form of brainwashing?................................10
Where did the science of meditation first develop?...........10
When did meditation come to the West?.............................11
What kind of meditation do you teach?...............................11
Aren't you biased? You only practice one type of meditation -
    how can you be objective about other methods?.............13
How do I know if this is the right meditation technique for me?...13
Do I need to have a Guru to learn meditation?...................14
What does meditation cost?..15
How much time does it take?..15
What are the benefits of meditation?...................................16
How soon will I feel something in my meditation?.............17

Chapter 2: Close Your Eyes..22

Taking a break..22
Sensory withdrawal...23
The lotus..26
Withdrawal symptoms...28
Fed up..30

Chapter 3: Concentration...34

The mind must have an object.......................................35
The inner tape recorder...36
Living in the future...37
Complicated people...38
Living in the past..38
As you think so you become...39
Living in the present...41
The mind can only think about one thing at a time......43
Concentration..44
Concentration in meditation...45
Unlocking the door to self-discovery...........................46

Chapter 4: Mantra - The Song of the Inner World.....50

Thinking of our own consciousness..............................50
The power of sound...52
Sound as the origin of all things..................................52
Sound and healing...53
Sound affects our emotions...53
Mantra and cakras...54
Vrtiis - mental propensities..56
Sanskrit - the language of mantras...............................57
Breathing...58
The meaning of the mantra...58
The power of thinking - your mental object.................59
The power of positive thinking.....................................60
Mental power...62
Beyond positive thinking..63
Exercise - what do you really want? 64
The ideation of the mantra..66

Chapter 5: Open Your Mind: Ego and Intuition 68

Faulty programming 70
Off course 73
I did it 75
Beyond the conscious mind 76
Intuition 79

Chapter 6: Karma 86

As ye sow, so shall ye reap 88
Don't complain. It's God's will 89
From the mind's eye 91
Yoga psychology 92
Making the unconscious conscious 95
The meditator's approach 97
Mindfulness 101
Good luck? Bad luck? Who knows? 103

Chapter 7: Open Your Eyes 106

Sentimental attachment 107
The evolution of sentiment 108
Relative truth vs. absolute truth 111
Law of karma and service 112
Love all, serve all 113
How to save the universe 116
The role of a spiritualist in the world 118
The beautiful revolution 120

Appendices:

A. Next Steps on Your Journey 123
B. Practical Tips to Improve your Meditation 125
C. Astaunga Yoga 130
D. Recommended Reading List 135

Glossary of Sanskrit Terms 137

About the Author 140

Introduction

"Your vision will become clear only when you look into your heart. Who looks outside, dreams. Who looks inside, awakens."

Carl Jung

In recent times meditation has attracted widespread interest throughout the western world. In 2003-4 Time magazine ran two front-page feature articles depicting Hollywood celebrities in a variety of meditation poses. We no longer have to go to an esoteric bookstore to find meditation books - every airport bookshop has them. A Google search for Meditation unearths twelve million pages, while a growing list of prominent public figures - Tiger Woods, Al Gore, Julia Roberts, Steve Jobs, Sting, Jennifer Lopez, John Cleese, Heather Graham, Richard Gere, Susan Sarandon and many more - make no secret of their meditation practice.

This is a far cry from the situation I faced when I learned meditation years ago. Eager for this ancient knowledge, I felt that I was venturing into unknown territory, leading to a world of new experiences; in 1975 hardly anyone in New Zealand had heard about meditation.

Nowadays it is hard to get a place in a meditation class in London or New York. The media portray it as something cool, so much so that marketing executives often use it to sell a wide variety of products and services. Advertisements for Phillips cameras, NatWest bank loans, Virgin Atlantic airlines and a host of others contain images of people in meditation poses. If someone sits meditating in a train or a park in London, hardly anyone turns their head. Times sure have changed.

So why has meditation become so popular?

1. It is practical. It is something we can do by ourselves, and we can experience the benefits first hand.

2. It promotes good health. A growing number of doctors and scientists recognise the beneficial physiological effects of meditation, especially in the areas of stress relief and relaxation. This has been so widely researched and documented that there is now little doubt that meditation has significant health benefits.

3. Meditation has received widespread coverage in the media. Sports people and health care professionals openly advocate meditation, and magazine editors and advertisers now portray meditation as a normal part of everyday life.

4. Meditation has been accepted as a part of popular culture. Meditation was first introduced to the Western world in ancient Greek times, nearly 3,000 years ago, but this knowledge was to a large extent lost over time. It was re-introduced to the Western world at the beginning of the 20th century, and European intellectuals were exploring oriental mystical philosophy, which has its roots in meditation, long before that. But it took the revolution in thinking of the 60's generation, and events like the Beatles taking up meditation, to create widespread public awareness of the practice. Now that same generation have entered middle age, and some of the values that they embraced during their youth have gained broad-based acceptance.

5. Nowadays we have access to vast reservoirs of knowledge from many cultures. We can choose from the best that a wide variety of traditions have to offer. People have sometimes asked me why I chose a spiritual practice originating in a culture other than my own. Just because something originates in another country does not mean it is unsuitable for us. Computer science was first developed in America, but no one suggests that computers are not useful elsewhere. Meditation originated in India and has been practised for thousands of years in Asia, but people from all backgrounds can experience its benefits.

6. Meditation is a way for people to explore their own spirituality. At a time when many people are disillusioned with institutionalised religion, meditation offers us a method to enter our own inner world, and experience spirituality directly.

Meditation is a practice

In spite of meditation now being widely accepted - it is even used in hospitals and taught in schools and by sports coaches - it is surprising how few people actually do meditation. How many people do you know who meditate every day? Many people think meditation is a good thing, and tell themselves, or me, as a meditation teacher, that they intend to try it one day. I've had people tell me that they believe in meditation. But they don't actually do it. This is like saying 'I believe in swimming', without ever going for a swim. We cannot experience the benefits of meditation by reading about it, or hearing about it, or philosophising, or listening to music by some rock star who used to meditate, any more than we can learn to swim from a book. A swimmer has to jump in and get wet. If we want to understand what meditation is, we have to practise it.

Although reading about meditation is no substitute for practising, it is important to understand the basics of what meditation is, and what it is for. In spite of the great amount of information available, there is still some confusion about this subject. In this book I've tried to explain the practice in a simple way, without losing sight of its deeper spiritual purpose.

A common reason people practise meditation these days is to relax. But relaxation is not the main purpose of meditation; it is just a side effect. This book focuses on what the sages of old felt to be the main purpose of meditation, the finding of one's 'Inner Self.' These sages developed their methods of meditation at a time when relaxation and stress management were not the primary concerns of humankind. Meditation thus has its roots in the knowledge propagated by sages living in ancient India. It evolved as a response to the human yearning to know the Inner Self - to know the mystical spiritual world, which we sometimes glimpse, but seldom grasp. Meditation is far more than just a therapy - it can bring spiritual fulfilment on a level beyond ordinary understanding. Who can comprehend the Enlightenment of the Buddha, or the ecstasy of the saints and yogis? These experiences take us far beyond ordinary thinking, and yet merely by virtue of being human we all have the potential to attain these highest spiritual states.

Self knowledge

When I was in Nepal in 1979 undergoing my training as a meditation teacher, we sat for meditation six hours a day. My mind became so clear and my concentration so sharp that I found that I could easily discern the inner meaning of difficult philosophy books. I felt that I already knew it intuitively. If we want to understand spiritual concepts, rather than studying intellectual ideas, it is best to practise meditation first to develop our intuition. First we need to understand ourselves. Then we will understand everything else more clearly.

"If you want to know all, know One, and that One is your own Inner 'I'."

Shrii Shrii Anandamurti

Spiritual understanding comes from inner knowledge and realisation. It is not an intellectual process. Some saints like Sri Ramakrsna, were illiterate, yet they had a deeper understanding of the ultimate truth than the greatest intellectuals or scholars. That is why this book is not about philosophy, and it is not about health or relaxation. It is about meditation practice - the key to higher awareness.

The first chapter addresses commonly asked questions. In chapters two to four, we will learn the basic techniques of withdrawing the mind, concentration and the use of mantra. The next two chapters explain some psychological and spiritual matters pertaining to ego, intuition and karma, the law of action and reaction in personal life. Chapter seven discusses the relationship between spirituality and worldly realities, and raises the question, "what do I do after meditation?"

There are different kinds of spiritual meditation, from a variety of traditions. I have not practised them all - far from it - so I cannot relate from my own experience the effects of all of these different techniques. Since it can take a lifetime to become adept in just one technique that would not even be possible. But I do not believe that this is a problem. If we are in a dry land, and need to dig for water, one hole is enough. But we must go deep. The digging of many shallow holes will not quench our thirst. The principles I describe here can be applied to any kind of meditation. The spiritual nature of human beings is universal, and the human mind has the same intrinsic characteristics the world over. It is not so important what style we practise. If it is an effective technique, and we practise it sincerely, it will help to satisfy our spiritual thirst.

Although this book is intended as a practical introduction to meditation, it is important to remember that no book is a substitute for a good teacher. If you would like to receive personal instruction in meditation, but do not have a teacher, I would encourage you to find one. At the end of the book, addresses and websites have been included that may assist you in your search.

Meditation brings about a change for the better. When I think of the way I have changed as a result of practising meditation, and of the way millions of others around the world have changed as well, I am filled with a great hope. It is clear that humanity needs a new vision. We need to change ourselves - and clearly there is a way to do it. Our meditation does not only benefit us. Our efforts create ripples that not only touch those around us, but spread outwards across the universe forever. And as people change, the world also changes. It is my hope that this book will guide you on your inner journey, as you walk the upward leading path, that finally we all must walk.

Dada Nabhaniilananda - London, 2006

"When we become interested in meditation, it is a sign that we are ready to take the journey to another level. As long as the journey remains an outer one, the real goal of our endeavours is never in sight. We continue looking out there for our destination, never realising that the 'I' that is doing the looking is what we are actually looking for."

Chuang-tse

Chapter One:

Start with Questions

*"The important thing is to not stop questioning. Curiosity
has its own reason for existing. One cannot help but be in
awe when we contemplate the mysteries of eternity, of life,
of the marvellous structure of reality. It is enough if we try
merely to comprehend a little of this mystery every day.
Never lose a holy curiosity."*

Albert Einstein

When we close our eyes and enter the private realm of our
own minds, we find ourselves in another world. Here
everything is different. Thoughts behave very different-
ly than things. True, there are images and memories from the outside world, but there are also feelings, sensations, ideas and experiences that originate within us, and these interact with our
impressions of the outside world to create an internal universe
with a unique terrain, governed by its own laws and offering
endless possibilities.

Long ago, yearning to uncover the mysteries of this inner
self, yogis developed the practice of meditation. Through the
mastery of this practice, it is possible to deeply understand the
inner self. But it can go further than that. Through meditation we
can gain control over our minds, transform ourselves, and realize
our true potential.

This book explains how meditation works, and how to practise it. We will begin by addressing a few commonly asked questions.

So what exactly is meditation?

Meditation has been described as a kind of concentrated
thinking, but this does not mean just any kind of concentrated
thinking. Concentrating on a pet rock or an ice cream is not medi-

tation. Meditation is the process of concentrating the mind on the source of consciousness within us. Gradually this leads us to discover that our own consciousness is infinite. This is why the goal of meditation is sometimes described as 'Self Realisation.'

What is self realisation?

The goal of meditation is to realize who we really are at the core of our being. The philosophy of yoga says there are two different levels to our inner self: our mental or emotional self and our spiritual self.

The mental self is sometimes called the individual mind. It is limited because it is strongly associated with our limited physical body and is the cause of the feeling 'I am this individual person' - our ego.

But our real sense of self-awareness comes from our connection to a wider, subtler form of consciousness. Yogic philosophy says there is a reflection of an infinite, all knowing form of consciousness within our minds. This Infinite Consciousness is unchanging and eternal, and is at the core of our true spiritual 'Self'.

When we identify with the small ego-centred self this is called relative reality, because that small self is prone to change and death. But when we realize that there is a subtler, permanent reality behind the relative one and we see that our true nature is pure unlimited Consciousness, this is known as Self Realisation.

What is the difference between meditation and yoga?

To many the word yoga means a series of physical exercises - stretching and tying our bodies into impossible knots. But these physical postures are only one aspect of yoga, known as 'asanas'. The physical postures of yoga are practiced for their health benefits, and because they help to prepare the body for meditation. Yoga is both a philosophy of life and a system of spiritual practice.* The word 'yoga' actually means union between the individ-

---

* To learn more about the complete yoga system, please see Appendix C.

ual self and Infinite Consciousness. Meditation is the most important practice in the yoga system and is the means by which this merger or union is achieved. So yoga is a system or science that enables an individual to develop themselves physically, mentally and spiritually, and meditation is the practice that makes the mental and spiritual development possible.

What is the difference between prayer and meditation?

Evidence of the existence of religion dates back more than 40,000 years. Early religions were animistic, believing that the forces of nature were beings or Gods, and later pantheistic, worshiping many deities, and assigning divinity to the invisible but powerful forces of nature that held sway over people's lives. These gods were feared and were appeased through prayer or sacrifice. As society evolved, people gradually realised that there must be a single guiding power behind all these forces of nature, and theistic religions emerged - the belief in only one God. But the relationship was still based on fear, flattery, appeasement and attempts to persuade God to grant favours to individuals. Some religious prayer still reflects this today.

Philosophically, praying to God requesting something or asking God to do something, even for someone else, is illogical. According to all the theistic scriptures of the world, God is an all-knowing (omniscient) and infinitely benevolent being ('God is love') who already knows if somebody's mother is sick, or someone is unhappy, and surely cares enough to do whatever is necessary to help them. Any concerns, or ideas we have originate with God anyway, so telling God how to run the universe seems inappropriate, to say the least.

In yoga philosophy it is said that since Infinite Consciousness has given us everything, we should not ask that Entity for anything. But if we have to ask for something, we should ask only for more love for God, which is known as devotion.

Prayer can take various forms. What I've described above is known as intercessory prayer - asking for God's intervention in our affairs. More developed forms of prayer include prayers of gratitude, worshipful prayer, contemplative prayer and meditative prayer. These can help to bring the worshipper closer to God

4

through cultivating devotion, the feeling of attraction towards the Infinite Consciousness. But as long as it is based on a dualistic conception of God, meaning that human beings and God are kept inherently separate, prayer cannot be considered meditation. Spiritual meditation places no limit on our realization. It is a non-dualistic practice, and its goal is to merge our inner 'I' feeling with the Infinite Consciousness.

I think it very likely that all of the great spiritual teachers practised some kind of spiritual meditation and initiated their closest disciples into this practice. This was their treasured 'inner teaching'. Often however, with the passing of time, this esoteric part of their teachings was lost or watered down, their later followers were left with only their outer teachings about morality and philosophy. But the key to realising what these enlightened individuals realized has always been, and will always remain, spiritual meditation.

Is meditation a science?

Science (from Latin scientia - knowledge) is most commonly defined as the investigation or study of nature through observation and reasoning, aimed at finding out the truth. The term science also refers to the organized body of knowledge humans have gained by such research.

Since the yogic approach to spirituality uses both observation and reasoning to get at the inner truth, it must therefore be a science.

Meditation has been described as 'Intuitional Science.' Extensive laboratory tests have demonstrated the physiological effects of meditation, but this only shows us its external effects. Even a recording of a person's brainwave patterns is just a measurement of physical electrical waves. It does not tell us exactly what they are thinking or feeling. The only real laboratory for testing meditation is the mind itself, and the results need to be experienced personally. Another name for this science is 'Tantra' - the science of spiritual meditation, which enables the practitioner to merge his or her unit mind into Infinite Consciousness.

What is spirituality?

Spirituality is that which concerns Infinite Consciousness.

First let me make it clear that 'spirituality' should not be confused with 'spiritualism', which is concerned with mediums, communicating with the dead etc. Spirituality concerns Infinite consciousness - the same ultimate Truth that was realised by the great spiritual teachers throughout history such as Buddha, Jesus, and Krsna. According to spirituality, the goal of life is to merge the individual mind into Infinite Consciousness, and the way to attain this is by practising spiritual meditation.

Is spirituality scientific?

The central idea of spirituality - that Infinite Consciousness is the ultimate reality - is common to most oriental and some occidental forms of mysticism. It is not so remarkable that this idea is widely accepted by mystics and philosophers, but in the last century many scientists have pointed out parallels between quantum theory and the mystical view of reality described in the ancient texts of Taoism, Buddhism and yoga.

Not only Albert Einstein but virtually all his contemporaries including Werner Heisenberg, Niels Bohr, Erwin Schrodinger and Max Planck, in fact most of the pioneers of modern physics testified to a belief in mysticism. When Heisenberg (discoverer of the 'Heisenberg Uncertainty Principle') went to India and met with Rabindranath Tagore, the Nobel prize winning poet and a great yogi, he was enormously relieved to find someone who didn't think his ideas were crazy. The ancient yoga philosophy seemed to be saying much the same thing about reality as the emerging Quantum Theory. This has been the subject of much discussion and many publications, particularly since the 1960s. This topic, though fascinating, is beyond the scope of this book. I will refer you to some of those publications for a detailed explanation.*

---

* Two good books on this subject are:
The Tao of Physics by Fritjov Capra
The Dancing Wu Li Masters by Gary Zukav

What is mysticism?

"The unending endeavour to bridge the gap between the finite and the infinite is mysticism."

Shrii Shrii Anandamurti

"The most beautiful and most profound emotion we can experience is the sensation of the mystical. It is at the root of all true science. Someone to whom this emotion is a stranger, who can no longer stand rapt in awe, is as good as dead. That deeply emotional conviction of the presence of a superior reasoning power, which is revealed in the incomprehensible universe, is my idea of God.'"

Albert Einstein

What is the difference between spirituality and religion?

The founders of all the great religions taught spirituality, yet religion and spirituality are not the same. When my own spiritual master was asked if he was trying to start a new religion he replied:

"I am not interested in religion. I am interested in human beings and the goal of human beings, and how to bridge the gap between the two."

Many religions may make the same claim, but the reality is that all too often the spirituality taught by the founder of those religions has been lost, or obscured by dogma and ritual. There are profound differences between the teachings of Christ and the practices of mainstream Christianity, between what Krsna taught and Hinduism, between the teachings of the Buddha and Buddhism. Over time, divisions have developed within religions, which have sometimes led to persecution and even war. When you look at the darkest periods of religious history, it is hard to believe that people could depart so far from the exalted teachings of their great preceptors. The original message was spiritual, but to varying degrees that spirit has been diluted or lost through mistranslation and misinterpretation, through the loss of spiritual meditation practices, through the attempts of less evolved individuals to cloak spiritual concepts in dogma, and through religions becoming religious and political institutions.

Within all the major religions there are mystical traditions that include many of the features of spirituality, but these are the exception rather than the rule. They do not represent mainstream religion, and in many cases have even been branded as heresy, and the propagation of such teachings has all too often been rewarded with persecution.

What we are left with in our various religions is a somewhat confusing blend of truth and dogma. If we wish to sift out the spiritual elements it is important to understand the real differences between spirituality and religious dogma. With the passing of time, these differences within mainstream religion have become increasingly distinct:

a. Spirituality is theistic, and has a highly developed and rational concept of God or Infinite Consciousness. Religious dogma can be theistic, as in Judaism, Christianity and Islam, or atheistic, such as Buddhism, Shintoism, and perhaps even communism. Dogmatic Religions generally have either a poorly developed and irrational concept of God, or no concept of God at all.

b. Spirituality is non-dualistic, and states that the purpose of human life is to merge one's self (or sense of 'I') into Infinite Consciousness. Theistic religions tend to be dualistic, propounding a fundamental separation between God and the world and the belief that the purpose of human life is to enter into a relationship with God and go to heaven after one dies.

c. Spirituality is practical, and can be experienced and realized by practising spiritual meditation. The focus is inward, taking the practitioner towards a personal realisation. Religions on the other hand, emphasise faith and belief, and though they teach people different types of prayer, most of the actual practice is externally focused, involving rituals, festivals and ceremonies.

d. Spirituality is a lifestyle choice, and is integrated into every aspect of a person's existence. Much Religion is ritualistic, and is generally a compartmentalized part of a person's life, practised primarily in temples and churches.

Religion can only serve it's proper purpose of liberating the faithful from ignorance and spiritual darkness, to the degree that it remains true to its original spirituality.

What is spiritual meditation?

In spiritual meditation our mind is directed towards a spiritual idea. The simplest way to conceive of this is to think of infinite love, peace and happiness, or an entity embodying that. We may call it God, but the name is not important. What is important is to remember that this infinite love is within us and surrounding us.

If we pause to consider, it becomes apparent that every experience we have ever had took place within our minds. If we want lasting happiness or love, what better place to look than at the source of these feelings?

Spiritual meditation is concentration on a spiritual idea, an idea associated with Infinite Consciousness, an idea that is greater than our selves. As we contemplate this vast and beautiful idea, our mind is transformed into pure consciousness that has no boundary.

So spiritual meditation is the effort to merge our sense of 'I' into Infinite Consciousness.

Do you have to be a monk to be successful in meditation?

Clearly not. Buddha was a monk, but Shiva* - regarded by many as the father of yoga, had three wives. (This was not unusual 7000 years ago). Swami Vivekananda was a monk, but my own Guru, Shrii Shrii Anandamurti, was married. And many great spiritualists were women, such as St. Theresa of Avila (a nun) and

---

* Shiva is also known as Sadashiva, or Lord Shiva and is regarded by many as the father of Yoga, the first great yogi. He is a historical per - sonality, but has since been deified by the Hindus who worship him as a god with four arms. I'm fairly certain that he really only had two arms.

9

Anandamayi Ma (who was married).

I chose to be a monk for both personal and practical reasons, but I certainly do not see it as any kind of pre-requisite for spiritual practice or success on the spiritual path.

Isn't it self-centred to sit around meditating all the time when there is so much suffering in the world?

I could be. It rather depends what you would be doing if you weren't meditating. If the answer is "watching television," by all means, meditate. But if it means you are neglecting your family, or using it as an excuse to avoid doing something for others, that is another matter.

I discuss this in detail in chapter seven.

Is meditation a form of brainwashing?

While it is no doubt true that the minds of some people could do with a good wash, I have to say that meditation is not a form of brainwashing. Usually when people express concern about brainwashing, they are afraid of losing control of their minds and being manipulated.

Meditation actually helps to protect us against having our minds manipulated by strengthening our willpower and making us more self-aware.

If you're seriously concerned about other people manipulating your mind for their own purposes, I suggest that the first thing you do is switch off your television, a device which is used to great effect by advertising companies, amongst others, to influence people's behaviour.

Where did the science of meditation first develop?

Tantric meditation was first developed by the tribes of South India 10-15,000 years ago, as an expression of their natural desire to understand their own consciousness. About 7000 years ago it was further developed by Shiva, the great yogi of ancient India. This practice has since spread and been absorbed into different mystical traditions, including yoga, Taoism, Sufism, Zen Buddhism and Tibetan Buddhism. Similar practices have also emerged in indigenous cultures.

When did meditation come to the West?

Meditation practices were introduced into Europe at the time of the ancient Greeks, some of whom travelled to the East and learned from Indian yogis and philosophers. Alexander the Great, a student of Aristotle, brought a yogi back with him from India to be his spiritual advisor. The great Greek mystic and social reformer, Apollonius, found wisdom in the East and was greatly revered for his spiritual power. He was an advocate of universal religion and propagated the idea of internal rather than external worship. Refusing to champion one popular cult against another, he declared that he "was concerned with the spirit rather than the form of religion."

The early Judaic and ancient Egyptian religions were heavily influenced by oriental mysticism, and many people believe that Jesus may have practised and taught a form of yogic meditation that he learned in India during the 18 years of his life that are unaccounted for in the Bible.

After the collapse of the western half of the Roman Empire in the fourth century, when most of the libraries of Europe were burned, yogic meditation practices died out in the West. Later both indigenous and Christian mysticism were actively suppressed, particularly during the dark period of the Inquisition. Europe became something of a spiritual desert, focusing its attention on intellectual and technological development, militarism, trade, exploration and conquest. Religious institutions started to take a greater interest in politics than in spirituality.

But in the 1890s a spiritual renaissance began in Western civilization with the reintroduction of oriental practices by Swami Vivekananda, the dearest disciple of the great Indian saint, Sri Ramakrsna. Vivekananda was the first modern yogic master to come to the West at the beginning of the twentieth Century. This period saw the emergence of the Theosophists and Rudolf Steiner's school of Anthroposophy as well as a growing interest in Eastern mysticism amongst European intellectuals like Carl Jung, Aldous Huxley, and Herman Hesse. After Swami Vivekananda others followed, and in the 1960's, interest in eastern spirituality exploded in Europe and America, quickly spreading across the globe, even as far as New Zealand. The most refined expression of this merging of cultures may be found in the writings of the great Indian mystic and philosopher Shrii Shrii Anandamurti, who was the first spiritual preceptor to create a harmonious blending of occidental rationality and oriental mysticism. He was the founder of the modern spiritual movement, Ananda Marga, meaning 'The Path of Bliss'.*

Although spiritual meditation originated in southern India in ancient times, its influence can be found in many spiritual traditions. Today it continues to address a universal human need.

What kind of meditation do you teach?

The nature of the object or idea you choose to concentrate on in meditation will dictate the outcome. Meditation can be done for spiritual growth, or for relaxation and stress reduction, or even for some other reason, such as success in a sport or a career. The distinguishing feature of all spiritual meditation techniques, as taught in the great spiritual traditions, is that the technique has at its heart the idea of Infinite Consciousness - it is the contemplation of the infinite.

In Tantric meditation the practitioner learns a personal technique through a process of initiation and is taught a mantra which is repeated mentally. He or she is taught how to withdraw the mind from the external world and how to concentrate internally. The primary goal of Tantric meditation is to merge the individual consciousness into Infinite Consciousness. This is the type of meditation taught in the modern Tantric school of Ananda Marga.

---

* To find out more about Ananda Marga please visit
www.anandamarga.org

Aren't you biased? You only practice one type of meditation - how can you be objective about other methods?

I may be biased - none but an enlightened soul is perfectly objective. I think the technique I am practising is the best, at least for me - otherwise I'd be doing something else. At the same time, it seems obvious that there are many paths to enlightenment - otherwise how could people from different traditions have attained Self Realisation? I try to keep an open mind, and from my study of a wide variety of teachings I have understood that there are common psychological and spiritual principles underlying spiritual practice. The extent to which these principles are understood and applied will determine the effectiveness of a technique in taking us forward on the path of spiritual progress.

For example, it is a widely accepted tenet of psychology that "as you think, so you become." If this principle is applied in spiritual meditation, it means we should concentrate on the idea of infinite consciousness. But if we have been taught since childhood to feel guilty, or afraid of God, this will make it more difficult to practice. If, on the other hand, we are taught that we are children of the Divine, and that our true nature is perfect and loving, then the feeling of bliss in meditation comes far more naturally.

It is not necessary to learn all techniques in order to grasp how they work. In any event it would not be possible in one lifetime - it is hard enough to master even one.

How do I know if this is the right meditation technique for me?

This is something you have to decide for yourself. If you come across a practice that makes sense to you, and feels right, I suggest you try it. If you then experience that it is bringing the kind of changes you feel you need, keep doing it. If you experience difficulties, be patient. Don't be too hasty to switch to another technique. You may face the same problem again, and be forced to realise that the problem was with you, not with the technique. If, after giving it your best shot, it still doesn't seem to be working, try something else. But don't keep shopping around forever - you should try to find a technique you're happy with and stick with it. Remember those holes we were digging for water? If you keep starting new holes you're going to get pretty thirsty.

Do I need to have a Guru to learn meditation?

The word Guru means 'dispeller of darkness', and really refers to the Infinite Consciousness acting as teacher and guide to individual souls. So since Infinite Consciousness is omnipresent, the real Guru is within us already.

When an individual has attained Self Realisation, they are often referred to as a Guru, because the Infinite Consciousness within them is able to act and speak without the distortions of ego. So they are able to play the role of a perfect teacher and guide to others.

In the Bhagavad Giita, Arjuna asked his Guru, Krsna, whether it was possible to attain enlightenment through the guidance of the Divine, inner Guru, without the assistance of a Guru in physical form. Krsna told him that it is not essential to have a physical Guru, but if you do not, it will probably take you about 10,000 times as long to attain enlightenment.

Thirty years ago, I wanted to learn meditation but I didn't know how to begin. I read some books on the subject, and with what wisdom I could glean from their pages I began to practice. Which means I wasn't teaching myself - I was learning from those authors. Indirectly, they were my first teachers, even though they were no longer alive. Soon I realised that I needed clearer guidance and I began searching for a living teacher.

The fact that you're reading this book indicates that you want information about meditation. All of the knowledge in this book comes, directly or indirectly, from a Guru. Practically all of the spiritual books of the world derive their ideas from great spiritual teachers - Gurus. If they don't, they should. Gurus are the pioneers on the spiritual path who go before us and light the way, guiding those who follow.

Some people are afraid that having a Guru means you have to follow someone blindly. This is a misconception. My Guru, Shrii Shrii Anandamurtii, often quoted an old scripture that says that if a child says something rational we should accept it, and if God Himself says something irrational we should discard it like a straw. Genuine spirituality does not deny rationality.

And what is the rational course when seeking self-knowledge? When we are entering the mysterious realm of consciousness, the most rational course is to take the advice of a guide who knows the territory well.

And this territory can, at times, but quite deceptive, and difficult to traverse. If you read about the lives of great saints and yogis like St Francis of Assisi, or Milarepa of Tibet, you will see that they all had to face many trials and tests, and transcend the temptations of pleasure and power in order to attain true greatness. At these higher stages on the spiritual path, the guidance of the Guru is more important than ever.

If you do not have the chance to meet personally with a real Guru (and they are few and far between) do not despair. It is possible to learn from a Guru through their writings, through learning of their inspiring example, and directly from people they have appointed to pass on their teachings and techniques. And through meditation it is possible to establish a personal relationship with your own inner Guru.

What does meditation cost?

Traditionally spiritual meditation has been taught free of charge and it is available to all, regardless of a person's economic status. Meditation is a subtle spiritual practice and no monetary value should be attached to it. To attach monetary value to meditation taints and degrades it.

Nevertheless, there is a price. To get results from meditation you have to put something into it - your own valuable time and effort.

How much time does it take?

I recommend that beginners spend at least 15 minutes twice a day in meditation. Later this can be increased to two half hour sessions. This will give a good result, though some people choose to meditate for longer periods and experience even greater benefit as a result. How much you get out of your meditation is directly related to what you put into it.

What are the benefits of meditation?

Extensive studies have demonstrated the physiological and psychological benefits of meditation, but I prefer to simply relate the benefits I've experienced personally from this practice:

a. I feel more mental peace.

b. I am much more emotionally balanced. I am a musician and I can tell you that this is a very real benefit for someone with a somewhat artistic temperament.

c. I am more creative. I have always practiced a variety of creative arts, and when I started meditation I felt that I'd tapped into a rich new spring of inspiration, ideas and insights. Many writers, musicians and thinkers report that their inspiration usually comes when the mind is quiet. It seems quite natural that the calming effect of meditation should give us easier access to the deeper, creative level of our minds.

d. I discovered a profound Sense of Purpose in life. I have a growing sense that all life is moving in a positive direction - towards greater awareness, towards a greater feeling of oneness and harmony. I feel that I am also a part of that same flow of conscious evolution.

e. Improved self-awareness. Introspective practice makes us more aware of our own motivations and qualities. This is not always a comfortable thing, but if we don't see ourselves as we really are, how can we improve? More often it is inspiring to discover the amazing potential within ourselves.

f. I have a developing sense of universal love. As I am more in touch with the source of my own consciousness, I am more aware of the consciousness in everything. I feel more love within my self, and greater love and compassion for others. This naturally helps me relate to others more easily.

g. I enjoy good health - I lead a very busy life - I travel frequently and there are constant demands on my time. Yet I do not suffer from the stress related illnesses that afflict many busy people. Meditation and the natural lifestyle associated with it are definitely a recipe for a long and healthy life.

h. Improved will power and concentration. Over the years I

have noticed my mind becoming clearer and stronger. If we exercise a physical muscle, it develops. The same is true of the mind.

i. I really enjoy meditation. Sometimes it is hard work requiring concentration, but when it really flows it can be intensely blissful - more blissful than anything else I've experienced. It is far better than taking drugs, or so I'm told.

j. I am happy. I don't suppose I'm the happiest man in the world, though I'm working on it. But I know that I am much happier than I was before I started on this path, and this feeling has grown over the years. I'm more emotionally balanced, more creative, I'm developing as a person, I sense a profound meaning in my life, I feel closer to God, closer to people, I feel more love. Of course I'm happier. I'd have to be crazy not to be!

How soon will I feel something in my meditation?

Here's what happened to a friend of mine.

In the early 1970s, Steve was a young man living in Auckland, New Zealand. He and his friends had become interested in meditation, and they all learned from a yogi, an acarya of Ananda Marga like myself. After learning meditation, Steve practised very regularly, for thirty minutes twice a day but he didn't feel any effect. After a week or two he began to worry and asked his teacher what was wrong. They discussed what he was doing, and the teacher reassured him and told him and that he just needed to be patient and keep practising.

Meanwhile, all Steve's friends were enjoying their meditation, and some were having nice experiences. He continued. After another two weeks he became really frustrated and came to his teacher again and said he was not sure if he could go on. The teacher told him, "We are having a weekend meditation retreat in two weeks time. I am sure that if you keep practising, and come to the retreat, something will happen."

Reluctantly Steve agreed to keep trying. He was afraid that if he gave up, his friends would ridicule him, so he kept at it but began to hate meditation. By the time the time for the retreat came around he didn't even want to go, but since he had said he would, he couldn't easily back out without looking like a failure.

The retreat was on Waihiki Island, and everyone had planned to meet at the ferry in the morning. Now it happened that Steve's house was infested with wood eating insects called Bora. Since he was going away, he planned to ignite a 'Bora Bomb' - a canister of poisonous gas which kills these insects and stops them eating all the wood; otherwise they will eventually make the house fall down.

So he put his luggage outside, lit the 'Bora Bomb', came out and locked the door. When he got to the bus stop he realised he had forgotten his wallet. Part of him thought, "Great! Now I'll miss the bus and I'll miss the ferry and I won't have to go to the retreat." But he thought he still had to try to get there in case he was interrogated by his friends, so he ran home. Then he had to wait for his breathing to slow, as the house was full of poisonous gas. By the time he had caught his breath, gone inside holding his breath, retrieved his wallet, and got back to the bus stop, the bus had gone.

"Good," he thought, "but I suppose I should try to hitch hike." He was confident that no one would stop as he had tried to do it before and never succeeded in getting a ride from this stop. So he put out his thumb. The first car stopped.

"Where are you going?" the driver asked.

"To the ferry."

"No problem, I'm going there too."

He was caught.

He arrived at the ferry just in time to meet his friends and then he was stuck on the island for a weekend meditating and chanting and eating vegetarian food, all of which he was now beginning to detest. His meditation was worse than ever and he was completely depressed. Everyone else was so happy and high and he thought maybe he was the only person in the world who could not meditate.

If they had not been on an island he would have left and gone home.

Finally the last meditation session of the retreat began, and he thought, "This is the last time I am going to meditate in my whole life. Fantastic!" They were all chanting so happily and he was thinking, "So what? Who cares? I just want to get out of here."

He sat down for what he thought would be the last meditation of his life. Within seconds after closing his eyes he had an amazing experience. He felt as if the top of his head had been removed and was open to the whole universe. He lost all awareness of his body and became lost in a blissful trance. Afterwards he felt overwhelmed and went up to people in tears saying, "It works, it works," like a fool. So that wasn't the last time he practised meditation after all.

A colleague of mine calls that my 'can opener story.'

So how soon will we feel something in our meditation? Everyone's mind is different, so it is difficult to answer this question precisely. Some people I know had an incredible experience the first time they sat for meditation. More commonly, people find it hard at first, and begin to enjoy it as they develop more concentration and mental stillness. Some, like Steve, have dramatic tales to tell. Others give up and never find out what might have happened if they had persisted just a little longer. One important thing to realize from Steve's story is that all those weeks when he thought nothing was happening during his meditation were actually an essential part of the process, and that a deep change was going on within him all along. It just took some time to come to the surface.

If we really want to know how long we will have to practise meditation before we too can taste its benefits, there is only one way to find out. The sooner we start, the sooner we'll know.

So let us close our eyes and open our minds, and accept that meditation practice involves an effort. If you undertake this wonderful practice with sincerity, I am sure you will long thank the day that you did.

"You can chase a butterfly all over the field and never catch it. But if you sit quietly in the grass it will come and sit on your shoulder."

Unknown

Chapter 2:

Close Your Eyes

*"Come away Oh human child
To the waters and the wild
And leave your cares behind...."*

W.B. Yeats

The desire to do meditation begins with our need to leave our everyday concerns and struggles behind and reach for something deeper, something quieter, something closer to who we really are. When we sit down to meditate, our daily worries and our ties to the external world are like strong ropes that keep our awareness moored to the docks of our mundane life. They try to prevent us from embarking on our voyage into the open waters of our inner being. So the first step on our journey is to cut loose the ropes and say farewell to the docks of the outside world. This process is known as sensory withdrawal.

Taking a break

Behind the need we feel to break away from it all lies an innate desire for the something more that we all long for but have never been quite able to find. Our endeavours and successes in the external world are important. They are the physical shape we give to our dreams and aspirations. But when we pin all our hopes on finding happiness or fulfilment 'out there,' we are likely to be disappointed, and when this happens we start looking for what is missing.

People find all sorts of ways to break away and enjoy a little freedom, if only for a few minutes or a few hours or a few days. It may be a weekend camping trip, a vacation in Hawaii, a concert, a party, a few hours at the local pub, or an evening lying in front of the television. All of these, and hundreds of other lesser or greater ventures, can satisfy our need to get away and leave our burdens behind us, at least for a time.

A love for art or nature can help us be more introspective. A piece of music may move us or a concert may transport our mind to some distant place that had seemed impossibly remote as we sat in the office or behind the wheel of the car, carving our way through traffic on the way home from work. Art can also do that. It can take us to realms inside ourselves that we normally find difficult to access; it can show us a glimpse of the interior landscape hidden behind the veils of our busy lives.

Nature too has that quality. There is a quietness in nature and a sense of vastness that reflects the depths inside us like a colourful mirror and helps us to connect in some way with our own limitless Self.

If you think for a moment of the many things you do to break away, you'll find that most of them represent an attempt to connect, at least for a while, to something deep inside.

"The objects of pleasure do not give us the happiness. The objects are merely keys to the happiness. They momentarily unlock the happiness that is always inside us."

Deshapriya

Sensory withdrawal

"Try to penetrate as deeply as you can into your mind, keep moving inwards but do not forget the realities of the external world, because if you ignore the external realities, your internal peace will also be disturbed."

Shiva

Our senses connect our mind to the physical world. They are like gateways that allow our inner awareness to perceive and communicate with the reality that exists outside us - gateways that can be closed or opened in order to regulate the flow of information. This link is made possible by millions of tiny chemical reactions in the central nervous system, which convert physical sensations into impulses that are carried by the nerve cells and nerve fibres. Electro-chemical charges jump across the gaps between neuron transmitters and neuron receivers, passing the signals along at incredible speeds. It is this constant electro-chemical activity which keeps the mind connected to the world, enabling us to function.

When the flow of stimuli that passes through the gates of the senses stops, we often experience a sense of freedom and peace. Most of the stress we feel in our daily lives is intimately connected to the flow of information we receive from the outside world. When that connection is broken for a time, we experience an exhilarating sense of lightness, as if our burdens had suddenly been taken from us. We feel relief from the tensions that are associated with the sights and sounds and other stimuli of our environment, hence the old adage "out of sight, out of mind". Since the early 1970s this phenomenon has been studied extensively by psychologists using sensory deprivation experiments. These studies include the use of so-called 'samadhi' tanks where the subjects are placed in an artificial environment that cut them off from almost all sensory stimuli. After spending prolonged periods in such an environment subjects report profound experiences of joy and tranquillity, and a sense of freedom from the cares of life.

Human beings have been finding ways to withdraw from their senses since the beginning of civilization; it is something that is deeply embedded in our racial memory, even if we are unable to explain it intellectually as a meditator or a psychologist might. During their initiation into manhood, young Native American boys would traditionally go on a vision quest, something common to many indigenous cultures. They would withdraw into seclusion in a lonely, isolated place and fast, meditate, ingest certain herbs and go for several days without sleep in an effort to disconnect themselves from the world they knew and enter the inner world in search of themselves. Similar practices exist in most religious traditions in one form or another; the seeker cuts him or herself off from the world, especially the world of the senses, in order to search for self-knowledge. It is not only ascetics and hermits who use such methods. We find tales of errant knights fasting all night and praying in the King Arthur stories.

Most of us respond to the need to withdraw from external stimuli instinctively. When we feel a need to get in touch with ourselves, we go off alone to a place where we won't be bombarded by the constant barrage of information that saturates our normal daily life. Often we take refuge in the peace and tranquillity of nature - that is a simple and effective way to slow the traffic entering the doors of our senses. Another widespread method of putting a temporary halt to our sensory input is the use of drugs and alcohol. What is actually happening when we drink a few glasses of wine to help us relax in the evening after a hard day, or get ourselves good and soused on a Friday or Saturday night so we can put the week behind us?

Biologically what happens is that the alcohol makes the lipid membrane of the nerve cell permeable, thereby deadening the nervous system. In cells where this occurs, the electrical impulse is lost.

Not all the brain cells are destroyed. Many just have holes in them for a few hours. Messages from the world of the senses do not get through, leaving us less and less aware of what is happening outside ourselves. An intoxicated person will be far less sensitive to the pain of an injury while under the influence of alcohol. One of our common expressions for being intoxicated is "feeling no pain," and it is not just a metaphor. We literally feel no pain due to the deadening effect of the alcohol. It is a kind of sense withdrawal. What we call a 'high' is nothing more than a temporary dissociation from the world of the senses. It is one way of 'taking a break' because alcohol creates a break in the pathways of the nervous system, the information highways of the mind. Drugs have a similar effect. They alter the way in which the information is passed along the nerve fibres thus disrupting our normal contact with the world around us.

Once we are disconnected from the world, we find that most of our cares and worries have been left behind, at least for a few hours. We are free to sing out of tune and dance and hug our friends and tell them how much we've always loved them. While some people experience bad reactions from drinking socially or using recreational drugs, for many people drinking and taking drugs is pleasurable. This is an indication that happiness is inside us. By helping us to disconnect, the alcohol or drugs help us to gain access to some of the happiness and peace within us.

Unfortunately, the heavy use of alcohol and drugs wreaks havoc on our body and damages our nervous system, as well as weakening the will power and creating physiological or psychological dependency, so over the long term their negative effects far outweigh any enjoyment we may derive from them.

Meditation also starts with sense withdrawal, but not by deadening the senses. It strengthens the nervous system and brings it under our control. Unlike artificial methods, it has no harmful side effects.

In meditation, sense withdrawal is accomplished by quietening the sensory organs and by bringing the mind to a point of concentration so that its connection to the gateways of the senses is suspended. Let us take a closer look at this process.

The lotus

The recommended posture for meditation is called the 'lotus' posture, not because we look like a flower when we sit in this position, but because of the characteristics of the lotus blossom. Lotuses grow in muddy, stagnant water yet produce one of the most beautiful flowers in the world. The name indicates that even while meditating in the midst of the trials and tribulations and stagnant water of the material world, we can rise above it by entering the stillness within, the land of unsurpassable beauty.

To sit in the lotus posture, you sit as if you are going to cross your legs, and then place your right foot on your left thigh, and your left foot on your right thigh. Straighten your back. To do meditation, fold your hands in your lap with your fingers interlinked. Close your eyes and curl your tongue backwards against the roof of the mouth. This posture allows you to keep your back straight and is an ideal posture for meditation, as it promotes concentration and calmness of mind.

Of course many beginners in meditation find it too difficult, in which case they can adopt the half lotus posture, where the right leg is rested on the left, or they can sit in the even simpler cross-legged position.

The benefits of sitting in the alternative postures are almost the same. If the cross-legged posture is still uncomfortable, sitting on a large cushion is recommended. The cushion should be large enough to allow you to sit in reasonable comfort with a straight back. And if this is still not possible, you can even meditate in a chair. For a beginning meditator, being reasonably comfortable and relaxed is more important than sitting correctly. You should certainly avoid forcing your body into an uncomfortable position.

The effect of sitting in the lotus is to turn the mind inward. When we sit in Lotus, or one of the other meditation postures, our sensory and motor organs become less active. We close our eyes so we can't see anything. We choose a quiet place to meditate so we won't be distracted by sounds. By folding our hands and crossing our legs, we cannot touch anything just like when a turtle withdraws inside its shell,. When the tongue is curled and pressed against the roof of the mouth, it deactivates the taste buds. If we have chosen our place well, we will also be not be bothered by smells. Simply sitting still in such a posture without moving is in itself a powerful aid to sensory withdrawal. By disengaging the mind from the senses, we are disconnecting it from the external world and giving ourselves an opportunity to dive deep inside ourselves. Motionlessness of the body leads to tranquillity of mind - simply by sitting still our mind becomes calmer. When we close the doors of the senses, we get the chance to explore what is behind those doors.

Sitting motionless with our spine straight in the meditation posture is a simple technique, but it is not as easy as it might sound. In fact, most people find it quite difficult at first. Neither our bodies nor our minds are used to it, and they may both therefore object in the beginning. Yet, with perseverance we can become adept at sitting quietly in the meditation posture for extended periods of time. Once we can do that, we will experience the power of these simple techniques to calm our minds and help us to advance on our inward journey.

Think of a rocket taking off. Most of the fuel is actually expended in the first few minutes in the tremendous effort required to overcome the forces binding the rocket to the earth and propel it beyond the earth's gravitational pull. But once that inertia has been overcome, and the rocket has reached its orbital altitude, it is able to travel great distances at high speeds with very little expenditure of energy. Meditation is much the same. Achieving escape velocity and breaking out of the gravitational field of our day-to-day conscious mind requires the application of great physical and mental energy. Keeping our spine straight and our body still may be quite difficult, but it helps the mind get the energy it needs for take-off. A straight back increases the flow of blood to the brain, which is very important during meditation, and it also helps us to take full deep breaths which increase the oxygenation of the blood. A straight back also stimulates the subtle vital force in the body which travels up the spine during meditation. This is called chi or ki in China and Japan (as in Tai Chi or Ai-ki-do), and prana in India. Learning how to concentrate the mind and prevent it from running around wherever it wants will be discussed in the next chapter. This will require even more energy. Without the expenditure of energy, however, the chances are that we will never leave the ground.

"Not once in a thousand times is it possible to achieve anything worth achieving except by labour, by effort, by serious purpose and by the willingness to take risks."

Theodore Roosevelt

Of course there will still be some interaction between your mind and the external world, while sitting in the lotus posture. After sitting quietly for a few minutes we may find that sounds and smells which we wouldn't ordinarily even notice start clamouring for our attention. If we find this happening, we may be experiencing the meditator's version of withdrawal symptoms.

Withdrawal symptoms

We are accustomed to receiving a constant flow of information through our sensory organs. This stream of stimuli keeps us company from the moment we wake up till the moment we go to sleep. Then we add our own flavour to the mix through a continuous inner dialogue of which we are only sometimes aware. When we sit down for meditation and try to turn all that off, we are doing something entirely unfamiliar, something contrary to our normal psychic processes. We are trying to suddenly change the habits of an entire lifetime. Faced with the unfamiliar experience of sensory deprivation, the mind instinctively wants to grab on to any stimulus it can, just as a person caught in quicksand tries desperately to grab on to anything solid. We may suddenly become hypersensitive to whatever sensory information does succeed in passing along our neuron pathways, which are, of course, still open …. information that ordinarily would never catch our attention. "Is that a phone ringing?" we ask ourselves when we hear some faint sound in the distance. "What could that smell be?" Suddenly we detect an unrecognisable whiff of something in the air. No sooner do we embark on our inner journey than our conscious mind feels uncomfortable with the unfamiliar quietness and wants to go back to what it knows best: paying attention to what is going on out there and thinking about it.

"I bet it was Sue. Maybe there's been an accident. I should have picked it up…"

"I think I hear Jack bringing in the mail. Maybe that application's arrived. With all the things I have to do, I can't sit here and meditate. I'll try another time."

Normally, thoughts run through our mind like a herd of wild horses. As long as they are untamed, they continue to do what they want, and going for rides with the help of our senses is what they enjoy most - meeting people, watching what's going on, enjoying the sights and sounds of a fascinating world. If we fence our thoughts in through a process of sensory withdrawal, they will rush to find an open exit. If they don't find an open exit, they may panic and try to jump the fence or squeeze through a small opening. This is the initial effect on the mind of the sensory withdrawal process. We quickly become aware of our craving for sensory input and at the same time we begin to discover how little control over our thoughts we really have.

If we think about it, this characteristic response of the mind when it first starts withdrawing from the senses is not much different from that of an addict deprived of whatever he or she is addicted to, be it food, drugs, applause, or whatever. Our minds have grown dependent on this sensory stimulation and, when deprived of it, crave it as an addict would. We have become hooked on the world outside us, and it is this that makes it so difficult for us to sit quietly for 20 or 30 minutes to explore our inner world.

On evening Mullah Nasrudin lost his keys somewhere inside his house. A little later a neighbour came by and found the Mullah crawling on his knees, searching in the grass under a street lamp outside by the road.

"What have you lost?" asked the neighbour.

"My keys," said the Mullah and continued searching.

"Here, let me help you," said the friendly neighbour. After a short time another neighbour came by and joined the search, and then another, until there was a small crowd of them crawling about. Finally the Mullah got up. "This seems hopeless," he said.

"Where do you think you lost the keys?" asked the first neighbour.

"In my house," said the Mullah.

"Then why on earth are we all searching out here under the street lamp?"

"How would we ever find them in the house? It's too dark - you can't see a thing. Out here there is a light," replied the Mullah.

Fed up

Sometimes we become addicted to external stimulation so that we experience sensory overload or sensory burnout. Think about all the people you know, and I'm sure you will find someone who can't go more than an hour without putting something in their mouth. For some it's a cigarette. For others it's coffee or snacks between meals. Often these are unconscious, compulsive actions, which stimulate and engage the sensory and motor organs. Being almost the only creatures that eat when they are not hungry, we humans soon become literally 'fed up'. Obsessive behaviours in other areas of our lives have a similar effect. Because we have not developed our inner resources, we feel the need to constantly feed ourselves with stimuli as a means to keep ourselves happy or at least stave off depression. But this dependency leads to a vicious circle that it may be difficult to break out of. We need more and more stimulation to get the same effect - the five cups of coffee becomes eight and the pack of cigarettes every day becomes two. The more we take in, the stronger our dependency, the less able we are to break away. This vicious circle can eventually lead to fatigue, anxiety, nervous disorders and mental breakdown.

"We have tested and tasted too much love
Through a chink too wide there comes in no wonder
But here ...
We will charm back the luxury of a child's soul."

W. H. Auden

Do you remember how good things used to taste as a child? How full of mystery and wonder the world was? But by the time we reach adulthood we have often become so accustomed to the objects of the senses that we are no longer able to appreciate the freshness, the mystery, the beauty of the world around us. The practice of sensory withdrawal gradually changes all that. It weans us from our dependence on objects of self-gratification and helps us gain control of our senses and root out our obsessions, restoring in the process the sense of wonder that we had as children. By recapturing the magic of a child's innocence, even the simple things in life can fill us with joy. Rather than denying the external world, meditation, through its practice of sense withdrawal, rejuvenates our senses; it restores our appreciation of everything, just as fasting for even a few hours gives us a healthy appetite and adds flavour to whatever we eat. When we finish our meditation we experience the beauty of the wonderful sights and sounds of this world with renewed interest, as though we had just come back from a holiday. And indeed we have.

But sensory withdrawal is just the beginning. It gives us a push to help us take our boat out of the harbour. If we are to sail out into the open waters of our inner being, will have to learn how to control our mind, and the key to unlocking the powers of the mind is concentration.

"...And I have felt
A presence that disturbs me with the joy
Of elevated thoughts; a sense sublime
Of something far more deeply interfused,
Whose dwelling is the light of setting suns,
And the round ocean and the living air
And the blue sky, and in the mind of man;
A motion and a spirit, that impels
All thinking things, all objects of all thought,
and rolls through all things...."

William Wordsworth

Chapter 3:

Concentration

"While doing meditation, the mind frequently runs after external things; it is extremely difficult to focus exclusively on only one object or idea. Why do we concentrate on a particular point during meditation? Because that point is the link between the relative world and the Absolute; the point exists where the relative world ends and the Absolute begins. It represents the Cosmic Entity. Once this point is controlled, the attainment of the highest state of spirituality becomes easy. Therefore in order to withdraw the mind from the relative world, we must concentrate on this point."

Shrii Shrii Anandamurti

Now that we have withdrawn our mind from our senses by sitting quietly in lotus (or cross-legged) posture, we can set sail on our voyage into the inner world. Sensory withdrawal weighs the anchor which ties us to our mundane lives and enables us to cast off.

But before we can even leave the harbour we find that we have brought a host of unruly thoughts on board, stowaways who are not the least bit interested in the voyage ahead. What they want is fame, fortune and a ripping good time, and prospects for that don't look good on this ship. So, like a band of rogue pirates, they try to waylay the captain. Not only do they fight against you, their would-be captain, but amongst themselves as well, each of them pulling your mind in a different direction. Heading into the sunset with this band of ruffians on board, you may begin to wonder what you have let yourself in for.

"A country can be conquered by force of arms, but the mind cannot."

Shrii Shrii Anandamurti

Let us have a closer look at this unruly mob of thoughts that plague our conscious minds. If we want to know how to deal with them, we must first understand their nature.

According to yogic science, the mind has three predominant characteristics:

1. The mind must have an object.
2. As you think so you become.
3. The mind can only think about one thing at a time.

Let us start with the first characteristic, and we'll look at the other two later in this chapter.

1. The mind must have an object.

It would be wonderful if we could just sit down in meditation and stop thinking altogether, without a single ripple in the mind to prevent us experiencing total peace and tranquillity. Unfortunately it is not so easy.

Try it for a moment. Close your eyes and try to make your mind blank.

Any luck? Even if for a few seconds you managed to avoid getting caught up in your problems, preoccupations or aimless thoughts, you would likely still have had some image in your mind - the room, your surroundings, the colours behind your eyelids. You would have had an awareness of yourself in those surroundings. You may have felt some emotion. Perhaps you were aware of your breathing. Almost certainly something was in your mind. If there wasn't, then there is no need for you to read the rest of this book or learn how to meditate, because you have already achieved what meditators spend a lifetime striving to achieve: Inner peace - the ability to make the mind completely still at will.

When the mind becomes completely calm, the meditator enters a state of bliss. Some adepts have, after many years of meditation, attained the capacity to enter this yogic trance at will, but such people are rare and they have achieved this only after years of effort.

We will discuss these higher states of mind later, but for now let it suffice to say that until one attains them there will always be a ripple in the mind. The mind must have an object. It must have something to think about if it is to exist in the first place. As long as your awareness of your Self or "I" continues to exist, the "not-I", what is outside your sense of self, will also continue to exist. This is the nature of the mind and there is no escaping it.

While for the time being you have no choice about whether or not you are going to think, you do have a great deal of choice about *what* you think about. Let us look at some of the things we normally think about and how they affect our mind.

The inner tape recorder

"You say so many things, and major portions of what you say are meaningless, simply a waste of time and energy. And not only that, but you also talk inside your mind. And that is a waste of energy too. Before going to Stockholm, you may say a thousand times in your mind, 'I have to go to Stockholm; I have to go to Stockholm; I am to go to Stockholm' a sheer waste of time and energy. What is thought? Thought means to talk in your mind. Thought is closely related to soliloquy. Suppose there is nobody to hear you and you are talking. What is it? It is just like a thought. When you are talking to yourself, it is called 'soliloquy'. Thought is also like that. Some of your thoughts are such that, if others hear them, they will say you are insane."

Shrii Shrii Anandamurti

If we observe our mind closely, we will find that we are talking to ourselves in one form or another all day long. Some of it is conscious, but much of it is sub-conscious, hidden just below the surface of our ordinary awareness. Sometimes we carry on conversations with people we know, or don't know; sometimes we have a discussion with ourselves. Often our fears and complexes get expressed through this internal dialogue, sabotaging our peace of mind. We sit down to take a test and tell ourselves that we can't possibly pass. We may not even notice that sub-conscious voice inside us, but it does its damage all the same. It is as though we had an internal tape recorder going 24 hours a day. We can't turn it off. We can't even turn the volume down. We may not pay attention to it all the time, but it is there in the background affecting how we feel and what we say and do. It can even get so bad at times that it seems as if we a re tuned into a radio station we don't like, but which we can't switch off.

Living in the future

Much of our mental energy is intimately bound up with our desires and aspirations, so many of our thoughts are concerned with an imaginary future. "If I can only pull off this job... I wonder what she'll be wearing... I hope it doesn't rain tomorrow, that would really spoil things... if I could just find a good teacher then I know I could make it," and so on. When our imagination is urged on by our anxieties or fears, we tend to think the worst rather than hope for the best. For every good reason to hope for success, the imagination finds several good reasons to expect failure and previews each of them in our internal cinema. "If this doesn't work out, then that's bound to go wrong. Then, Oh My God! I don't even want to think about what might happen then." But of course we do.

Although we sometimes think that our predictions of the future are accurate, they are often more like science fiction, and we spend much of our time and mental energy writing and rewriting that piece of fiction, a work which will never be published. Compared to the fantastic creations of our imagination, what actually happens may seem boring or commonplace. Our imagination makes difficulties the size of a golf-ball into colossal avalanches. Yet, in reality, most of what we think will happen, never does; the future has the habit of summarily destroying the "best laid plans of mice and men".

"My life has been full of the most terrible tragedies, most of which never occurred."

Dale Carnegie

Complicated people

One consequence of this living-in-the-future mentality is that people begin to live their lives as if the present had little importance except as a preparation for the imagined future. Young people want to get older, and older people wish they were young again. Personalities become strangely fragmented. A politician can think one thing, say another, and do something completely different in order to get elected. It is the same with us. When we consider what we say and do from the perspective of what benefit might result, we become complicated. We lie to others and to ourselves, seldom saying what we really feel for fear of the consequences it might lead to.

"Suppose your boss arrives. You welcome him saying, 'Please come in, sit down and have something to eat.' You flatter him externally, but inside you say, 'What a nuisance he has arrived! When will he go?' Your boss does not know this. Thus, you have two 'I's inside you: one performs actions in the external world, while the other thinks something different inside. You are well acquainted with this inner 'I', but others do not have a correct perception of it.' 'This is what we call the two faces of a single personality, a psychic disease. The greater the gap between these two 'I's, the more psychic torment a person will suffer. You must remember that in this second half of the 20th Century there is a great gap between the internal 'I' and the external 'I'. And because of the trouble in adjusting these two 'I's there is an increase in the number of lunatics. This is the greatest disease of the 20th Century."

Shrii Shrii Anandamurti

Living in the past

When our minds are not engaged in thinking about the future, we usually dwell on the past, and this tendency increases as we get older. Some of our memories are pleasant but some are inevitably painful, and often it is these painful events which we brood over the most. "She had no right to speak to me like that...It's his fault that everything is going wrong, I know it...I wish I had never done that; now look at the mess I'm in." If we feel we have been wronged we will usually find ourselves explaining our side of the story to someone else. But of course there is no one there. It is only the ravings of our inner soliloquy, as if we were rehearsing our lines before an empty stage. Or we waste our time replaying events and emotions in our heads over and over again like a television junkie watching re-runs of Dallas. Painful events of the past can even become an important part of our self-image, effectively barring us from a healthy, joyous experience of our daily life, even though they have no more substance than a mirage in a burning desert.

As we discussed above, the first characteristic of the mind is that it must have an object. We have to think about something. By now you have probably realized that what we think about has a great effect on our lives. You will thus have already stumbled across the second characteristic of the mind:

2. As you think so you become.

"Your imagination is your preview of life's coming attractions."

Albert Einstein

"Imagination is the beginning of creation. You imagine what you desire; you will what you imagine, and at last you create what you will."

George Bernard Shaw

The power of our thoughts to shape our reality has been recognized for thousands of years by the great thinkers of all cultures. Thoughts not only shape our reality, they are our reality, for it is through the mind that we experience the external world. All the brilliant inventions of mankind, both for good and for evil, began as seeds in the imagination and took birth when the mind turned those seeds into physical reality. The mind is the creative force behind all our achievements. Thoughts are not simply idle mental gossip; they are powerful creative forces which seek expression in the external world. If you look deeply into the world of events and objects in which you live, you will find someone's thought at the root of everything, from the red light that orders you to stop your car in the morning to the stroke of bad luck you meet up with in the evening which you swear was an accident.

Our attitudes colour our experience. They dictate what we see and what we don't see, hence the old adage that if a saint is walking down the street, a pickpocket will only see his pockets. Thoughts guide us down the road of life as we struggle to materialize our hopes and desires, and, if our thoughts are strong enough or persistent enough, they become the landscape through which our road passes, although what we get is not always quite what we bargained for. Most importantly, our thoughts are responsible for who we are, for our weaknesses and our strengths, our foibles and talents, our capacity to love, to endure suffering and to derive joy from the moment to moment drama of our existence. It is as the Buddha said:

"We are what we think, having become what we have thought."

The increasing emphasis on positive thinking that we see in Western society today is based on this second characteristic of the mind. If we indulge in negative thoughts, we develop negative tendencies of mind, and this not only creates anxiety, tension and fear, but it sabotages our efforts to get ahead in the world. By consciously striving to think positive thoughts, we increase our sense of well-being as well as creating a congenial environment for the materialization of those thoughts in our daily lives. A good example of this is the work of Mary Baker Eddy who successfully demonstrated the power of positive affirmations in the healing of disease. Now in order to utilise this second characteristic of the mind to our advantage, we will have to exercise some control over what we think. We will have to train the mind to keep it from getting lost and taking us where we don't want to go. An untrained mind is like a frisky young dog that dashes around madly the moment you let go of the leash. If we let the mind wander according to its natural tendency, it will pull us in many different directions, leaving us dizzy and confused, at the mercy of whimsical thoughts and conflicting desires. Thoughts generally concern themselves with an imaginary future and a dead but unburied past. If we are to train the mind properly, one of the first things we need to learn is to live in the present.

Living in the present

One morning I sat at the breakfast table watching a friend of mine gulping down his toast and coffee, reading the newspaper, and putting on his coat all at the same time. Every few seconds he would glance up anxiously at the clock and mumble something about how late he was going to be for work. When I asked him how breakfast was he had nothing to say except that he was "on his way out." "Was there anything interesting in the paper today?" I asked. "Don't know, he replied. "Take it. I'm out of here."

Yet 'here' was where his life was taking place. I thought it a shame that at that precious moment he should choose to be marked absent. Not to be able to taste the food he was eating or take in the headlines he was reading because he was mentally "on the way out." His body was going through the motions but his mind was elsewhere. He might as well have been eating the newspaper.

Later that day I watched the Spanish Formula One Grand Prix on TV. It was the most exciting race I had ever seen. About a third of the way through the race Michael Schumacher was way ahead of the field; then suddenly he slowed down and the other cars started passing him. His pit crew told the commentators that he was stuck in fifth gear. Rather than give up and pull out, however, Schumacher called in to the pits that he wanted to finish the race so that he could gain points for the world championship. Incredibly enough, after ten laps, he started to overtake the other cars and as he approached the final lap he moved into second place.

The television commentators could not believe that he was driving with only one gear. If he were, then how could he possibly be picking up speed out of the turns? They decided to stop their running commentary to let us all listen for a change of gear via the live video camera mounted on Schumacher's car. For the next half lap millions of people throughout the world saw and heard just what Schumacher was seeing and hearing as he hurtled down the straightway at breathtaking speed and into the turn.

There was no change of gear. I sat on the edge of my seat looking out of Schumacher's car as it flew into the turn at 150 miles per hour. With no gear change to help him slow down, his car wavered, almost uncontrollably. I could feel the excitement and exhilaration, almost as if I were sitting in the car with him, and the tremendous courage it took to be doing what he was doing.

Whatever Schumacher was thinking of as he hurtled down the straightway at 200 miles an hour, it was not dinner or even the next race or his next public appearance. Riding into the wind on a fragile piece of metal, he was focused on that moment as if his life depended on it, and it did.

> *"I must have waited all my life for this*
> *moment... moment... moment..."*

> Jon Anderson

It is only here, in this precious, fleeting moment that we are truly and fully alive. That fraction of an instant, the eternal 'now', which lies in the gap between the past and the future, comes and goes so swiftly that most of us miss it. Yet if we are fully awake at that instant, we find ourselves immersed in an experience so rich that no creation of our imagination can begin to equal it. It is only when we are fully awake in the present that we experience the vastness that life has to offer.

If Schumacher had not been fully present, mentally and emotionally, during his dramatic run to the finish line he would not have survived. Our situation is not as different as we might think. If we cannot be truly present as our life unfolds, we also will not survive; we will join the ranks of the living dead and we will miss out on what we came here for. Truly speaking, we are only alive to the extent that we are mentally present in our lives.

> *"Life is what happens to you while you're busy making other*
> *plans."*

> John Lennon

When, through the practice of concentration and meditation, we learn to discipline our mind and keep it from brooding over the sins of the past or wasting our precious energy on the phantasms of an imaginary future, we start to feel a tremendous sense of power. We feel more awake, more alive and uplifted. We become conscious participants in our life, awake to the infinite possibilities inherent in the moment. Whatever we choose to do, we do wholeheartedly with full attention. Then, no matter how mundane it may seem, even if we are only doing the laundry, it becomes filled with the joy and vitality of conscious living. The better our concentration becomes, the more the gap between what we are doing and what we are thinking starts to disappear. We begin to feel the oneness of all things.

> *"Oh body swayed to music,*
>   *O brightening glance*
>   *How can we know the dancer from the dance?"*
>
>   W. B. Yeats

The secret behind living in the present is the secret of true concentration. In order to understand how concentration works, both in meditation and in our life in general, let us look now at the third characteristic of the mind:

3. The mind can only think about one thing at a time

The mind must have an object, that is, we must think, and what we think about has serious consequences, both for ourselves and for the world around us. Now the third characteristic of the mind is that it can think only one thing at a time. This can be considered a limitation of the mind but it is also its great strength. It is because of this characteristic of the mind that concentration is possible.

Try as you like, you cannot make two thoughts occupy the same mental space at the same time. You cannot hold two different images in your mind at the same time or repeat two different words. Though we sometimes seem to be able to do so, what is actually happening is that the mind jumps from one thought to another at incredible speed. The effect is somewhat like that of a motion picture which is composed of a series of stills changing so rapidly (24 to 30 frames per second) that the objects appear to be moving. Science has discovered that all perception, whether visual, auditory, or whatever, functions in the same way, as a series of discrete "snapshots" that only appear to be continuous because of the minuteness of the gap between them.

Now let us see how this characteristic of mind affects the practice of concentration.

Concentration

Try going back in time to your school days and see if you can remember a student in your class who couldn't concentrate. Every classroom has one. The teacher would be discussing the fall of the Roman Empire and he would be sending notes to a friend at the back or fidgeting with his pencil or turning around at the slightest sound. No matter how often the teacher would ask him to pay attention, it would never last. A minute later his mind would be wandering again, or a sound or a movement from one of the other students would distract him. Do you remember such a student? Well that student was you and it still is. How often does it happen that while you are talking to friend you are actually thinking about the concert you have tickets for that evening - the one you've been looking forward to all week. Or you are sitting in the office listening to a colleague's presentation and your mind wanders off to a conversation you had at lunch. Or you're sitting in the concert and by midway through the second song instead of really listening to the music, you're imagining yourself onstage with the guitar in your hands and the audience going wild. The mind simply can't stay put, no matter how much we might like it to.

Some people do have it. A boyhood friend of mine had an amazing capacity to become absorbed in a book to the exclusion of all else. His sisters and I used to make a game of it. We would start talking about him loudly, insulting him and laughing and trying to make him notice us, but he was totally oblivious. He was so focused that he couldn't hear us.

So what is concentration? It is as simple as giving your full attention to one thing and keeping it there, be it that absorbing book, a friendly conversation, an inspiring piece of music or the beauty of the sun setting over the ocean; it is simple, but by no means easy. If you can concentrate, you have mastered the secret of living in the present, for when you are able to give your whole attention to what you are doing, you become fully awake in the moment. Your inner 'I' and your outer 'I' become one and your mind acquires tremendous power. In its ordinary scattered state it is just like the diffuse rays of the sun, warm but not particularly powerful. But concentrate those sunrays through a large enough magnifying glass and they can burn a hole through stone.

Once in Los Angeles, Paramahansa Yogananda, the great Indian yogi, was accosted by an armed robber who ordered him to hand over his money. "Put that gun down immediately," Yogananda said, and his words had such force that the robber threw down his weapon and fled. Someone with a concentrated mind is able to command more than just respect.

The basis of all meditation, and indeed of all conscious life, is the art of concentration, the capacity to focus our attention on one thing. When the object of concentration is our awareness, the infinite Self within all of us, that is meditation and the deeper our concentration, the more we are able to penetrate the secret of who we are.

Concentration in meditation

In meditation we turn the third characteristic of the mind to our advantage. Since the mind can only think of one thing at a time our task is simple. As long as the mind is engaged in one thought it cannot think about anything else. If it is engaged in the present it cannot get lost in the past or the future. Then all we have to do is repeat the same thought over and over again, like an hourglass with single grains of sand falling through, one after another, in a steady unbroken flow.

The way meditation accomplishes this is to choose a focal point for concentration. When the mind wanders away from its point of concentration, we bring it back. It wanders away again, and again we bring it back. We don't try to force it to remain focused by pushing other thoughts away, nor do we let it wander freely. We simply bring it back to our point of concentration once we become aware that it has wandered away, time after time, session after session, day after day. Over time the mind will develop the habit of returning to this point of concentration.

In the beginning it may only stay focused for very short periods of time, a few seconds perhaps, depending on how easily we can concentrate, and it may drift for some time before we even notice that it has wandered. But each time we bring it back we strengthen the habit. Gradually, due to the forced repetition, the mind becomes accustomed to this practice. The gap is reduced; we catch the mind much sooner when it does wander. Eventually we develop the ability to focus on our point of concentration for long periods of time. Distractions still come and go but they lose their hold over us. They lose their ability to divert our minds from what we are concentrating on. When the mind develops this ability to maintain its concentration it develops the tremendous force that allowed Yogananda to put to flight a would-be robber with a single sentence.

Now this technique of concentration can be practised with virtually any object as a focus. It can be something external like a candle flame, a spot on the wall, or something internal like a particular image or a particular sound. However, as we learned when we looked at the second characteristic of the mind, "as we think so we become," so our choice of what to concentrate on is vitally important. We are free to choose anything we want to concentrate on, but our choice of what we concentrate on will determine to a great extent who we become in the process. For concentration to become meditation, our focus of concentration must be our Inner Self, the goal of our long voyage through life. In the next chapter we will take a closer look at how we accomplish this.

Unlocking the door to self-discovery

One natural aid to the art of concentration is to choose something interesting to concentrate on. If you find that the movie you are watching is boring or if the conversation turns to a topic you have heard a hundred times before, it will be more difficult for you to keep your attention fixed on it. When we meditate we choose what is, for all of us, the most interesting thing in the universe. If you are shown your high school class graduation photo, who will you look for first? We all know the answer to that question. We are and have always been the real object of our search. Self-discovery is what meditation is all about because self-discovery is what the journey of life is all about.

In the beginning, meditation is a little like watching the ocean when it has been stirred up by a storm. The water is murky and laden with silt and mud, and we cannot see into its depths.

We cannot even see how deep it might be. But if we are patient, the mud slowly clears, and the vast undersea world with all its wonders reveals itself to us. In the depths of our own minds lies hidden the secret of who we are, our innermost and as of yet undiscovered Self.

When I was relatively new to the art of meditation, I learned something about how concentration can help one's meditation practice. I was on my way to teach an introductory meditation class, and I had about 2 hours to spare. I was near a beautiful beach in Noosa, Australia, and it was approaching sunset, so I decided to meditate on the beach. It was an idyllic spot. Small waves were breaking gently on the sand, and dolphins were playing in the water. It seemed like a perfect setting.

But no sooner had I closed my eyes than I felt a tickling sensation on my hands and then on my arms and face, and an unpleasant pricking on several spots of my exposed skin. Mosquitoes! I opened my eyes and to my dismay saw about a dozen mosquitoes beginning to feed on me and a cloud of about fifty more hovering nearby. How ironic that this perfect spot had to be infested with these bloodsuckers. I tried to brush them away and meditate anyway, but they were not at all discouraged, rather their friends began to gather around too. This was hopeless! I was not getting any meditation done at all.

So I took a firm determination that I would close my eyes and meditate for one hour without moving even if the mosquitoes sucked me completely dry. It was incredibly difficult at first. In my mind's eye I visualised them poking their terrible little noses into my flesh and drinking my blood. I was desperate to react, but I steeled my will and started my meditation. After a few minutes I found myself deeply absorbed in one of the most blissful meditation experiences I have ever had and thought no more of the mosquitoes for the next hour. When I opened my eyes, the mosquitoes had gone, and I was amazed to find that I had no bites.

I realised that I could concentrate anytime if I really wanted to.

With the Inner Self as our object of concentration we turn our mind inwards. As our experience of meditation becomes more blissful, our mind is naturally attracted to this mysterious Inner Self. Gradually, through regular practice, the stream of our consciousness gets focused in this direction. All our emotions and thoughts flow together towards the vast inner regions of the mind. When this happens, we experience a profound sense of inner joy, wisdom, peace and clarity, far deeper than anything we have ever known. From the conscious mind to the subconscious mind and deeper still, concentration in meditation is the key which unlocks the door to that wondrous inner Self.

"You opened new doorways,
shining on the world
I beheld You in the heart of dreams
This time the magic will never die."

> From the song *The Return of the Magic* by the author

Chapter 4:

Mantra - The Song of the Inner World

"Without depending upon mantra ... Buddhahood cannot be attained."

Dalai Lama

Thinking of our own consciousness

Imagine a countryside scene at night. It has been raining, but the clouds have cleared, revealing the moon. In its light a few cows saunter by. They leave footprints in the soft earth, and as water fills the indentations, they form a series of tiny pools with the moon reflected in each one. There appear to be many moons, yet anyone who looks up at the sky will understand that they are all simply reflections of the one moon.

We all feel that our 'I' feeling, our spark of awareness, is unique and different, yet many people have found that if they go deep enough into their inner mind, they realize that their consciousness is simply a reflection of the One Cosmic Consciousness.

This pure 'I' feeling, independent of any thought, is what we are trying to attain in our meditation. But how can we possibly meditate on consciousness, on something that is infinite, indefinable and beyond thought? The only thing that the eye cannot see is the eye itself; in the case of the mind, it is the 'I' that cannot see the 'I'; it is infinite and by definition inconceivable. How can the mind conceive of the inconceivable? How can the mind reach that which is beyond the mind, out of which the mind arises? This is the meditator's dilemma.

"A man does not seek to see himself in running water, but in still water. For only what is itself still can impart stillness unto others."

Chuang-tse

Spiritual meditation can lead us to the blissful domain of our deepest Self, which is the goal of our journey through life. If we want bliss, if we want happiness, if we want freedom, we must meditate on that which is ever blissful, ever happy, and ever-free. There is only one place to find this: within ourselves. Our object of meditation is consciousness itself, the infinite source of all things.

"A blade cuts things
but not itself:
Eyes see everything
but themselves."

A Zen Forest.
Sayings of the Masters
Translated by Soiku Shigematsu

Many thousands of years ago yogis in India discovered the solution to this ancient dilemma. They found a method that would help them transform the busy, uncontrolled mind into a translucent pool of peace. The method was mantra.

The word mantra comes from ancient Sanskrit. Mantra literally means 'that which liberates the mind'. Man means 'mind' and tra means 'freedom', so a mantra is a word or a group of several words which, when meditated upon, leads the mind to freedom. It can transport us through the maze of our thoughts to the ocean of pure consciousness. Now let us take a look at how it does this.

We must think about something when we meditate, that is, we must have an object to concentrate on. In this case, it is a word, a meaningful sound vibration that has the capacity to create a certain type of rhythm in our mind. All mantras used for meditation have three characteristics: sound, meaning and rhythm. Let us look now at each of these three characteristics in turn and see what they signify in the context of mantra meditation.

1. The power of sound

As I write these words I am listening to a recording of a spiritual chant by one of the finest musicians I know. The effect is mysteriously potent. With no effort on my part the music awaken a blissful feeling in my heart, soft but joyful. It is so strange - as a yogi and a musician, I understand the theory of why this is happening, yet the power of these sounds to transform my mood in a moment still seems magical to me. How can such a simple thing have such a powerful effect?*

Sound as the origin of all things

The mythologies of many different cultures tell us that at the Dawn of Time there was sound - that the Creator used music to weave a cosmic spell. The Christian Old Testament says, "In the beginning was the Word." Australian Aboriginal tradition tells how the Universe was sung into being, and in the Tibetan book of the dead the essence of reality is described as "reverberating like a thousand distant thunders."

In yoga philosophy the first vibration, the primordial sound of the Universe is known as the Aum (or Om) sound. This sound represents the sum total of all of the vibrations in the universe, embodying within it the three aspects of God as Brahma the Creator, Vishnu the Preserver and Maheshvara the Destroyer. In deep meditation it is possible to hear this sound, the Om sound, the seed sound of the entire Universe reverberating in our innermost being.

According to physics the universe began with a vast explosion of energy - a Big Bang. There are many parallels between creation myths and the emerging discoveries of modern physicists.

Vibration has great power - remember the biblical story of the walls of Jericho being brought down by the blowing of trumpets? When soldiers cross a bridge they are ordered to fall out of step to prevent the regular rhythm of their marching from setting up a resonance that could cause the bridge to sway higher and higher until it breaks.

---

* I was listening to the second track from the album Flow of Love by Sukha Deva. (Available from www.eternalwave.com)

Sound and healing

There are numerous instances of music being used in healing. Democritus of Greece wrote in the 5th Century BC of "snake bites being cured by the sound of a flute when played melodiously and skilfully." In the USA and Europe special therapy centres are using music to help Alzheimer's, Parkinson's and cancer patients. Music therapists are employed in many US hospitals with very positive results. Music producer, Terry Woodford, has made tapes using human heartbeats blended into the rhythm of the music which are used in more than 4000 hospitals and children's wards.

We see the same principle at work in the magical rituals and practices of indigenous people, in tribal chanting and in "magical spells", as well as in the many forms of religious chanting and music. In India there is an ancient tradition of healing through music, and incredible tales are told of mortally ill patients being cured by a musician playing a violin.

There is a story of the great Indian musician, Tansen, who, in order to please his king, caused a tree to burst into blossom out of season by playing a particular raga on his veena (a multi-stringed classical instrument, a little like a sitar).

Music is used in most spiritual or religious traditions to induce devotional trances, ecstasy, and altered states of consciousness.

Sound affects our emotions

We are very sensitive to sound. When we are in the womb as an embryo the ear is the first sensory organ to develop and it is fully functional four and half months before birth. Sounds heard in the womb stimulate the development of the nervous system. We have all experienced the capacity of sound to effect changes in our mental state. The sound of the sea is sometimes melancholic; the sound of a flowing river makes us feel serene, while the sound of a chain saw sets our nerves on edge. A Bach prelude, a baby crying or someone scraping their nails on a blackboard all affect our mind in distinctly different ways. Different sounds can induce completely different emotions in us, almost instantaneously. The same is true for form and colour. Sit quietly for some time in a light blue room then move to a bright red room and you will notice a marked change in your mental state. This is why mental health centres are usually painted light blue, or light green. It is hard to imagine anyone painting them red or black.

Everything that we perceive has an effect on the mind, and it is this fundamental universal law that makes the use of mantra so effective.

Mantra and cakras

If you go out in the countryside at night in clear weather, you will be dazzled by the brilliant light of thousands of stars scattered like jewels upon the ocean of the night. Yet the next morning they are gone. The sky is blue. We know the stars are there but the sun, so much nearer, outshines them.

Not everything that is real is visible all the time. We will never see some things that are real, like the wind, or the electromagnetic field surrounding the earth, or people's thoughts.

If we go down to the deep, quiet part of the mind, we will begin to experience its hidden wonders and we will start to understand much of our inner world. As the ancient yogis observed how different sounds affect our thoughts and feelings, they developed a subtle intuitive understanding of the relationship between different sounds, the body, the vital energy of the body and our mental state. Studying the body and mind, they gained many insights in the areas of health, psychology and spiritual practice. On the basis of this they developed the science of Mantra.

According to the yogic model, our physical body is just one aspect of the multi-dimensional human system. Parallel to the physical body is a more subtle body of vital energy or prana ('chi' in Chinese philosophy). The flow of this vital energy throughout our system regulates our health, our vitality, our thinking and our emotions. This is not a physical force - you will not find it if you cut open the body, but it flows in definite patterns in the body, and can be felt if we develop the right sensitivity. There are three main channels of vital energy. One runs through the centre of the spinal column. The other two originate behind the nostrils and in their downward flow they weave back and forth across the spine; the points where they intersect are known as cakras (or chakras). The seven major cakras are located in the vicinity of major glands

Diagram of chakras, nadis and vrtis of the human system. Illustration by George Azzopardi.

that influence our emotions through hormonal secretions. It is this cakra system that forms the connection between our physical bodies, our nervous system, our glands, and our minds. The third cakra for example, near the adrenal glands at the navel point, is related, amongst other things, to hunger and fear.

In high states of meditation this subtle energy body can actually be perceived as a pattern of brilliant channels of energy and glittering coloured lotuses along the spinal column at the points where the energy channels intersect. Each lotus petal corresponds to a particular human propensity, desire or feeling, and each has a corresponding colour and sound.

"The best and most beautiful things in the world cannot be seen or even touched. They must be felt within the heart."

Hellen Keller

Vrtiis - mental propensities

Our mental activity sometimes seems like an enormously complex matrix of desires and feelings, but the process through which thoughts arise is not random. At the core of our psyche are fifty principle propensities (vrttis in Sanskrit). Each emotion or desire we feel, such as fear, anger, compassion, affection or shyness - is the expression of one of these propensities. Some are mundane physical desires based on survival instincts. Others are more subtle, reflecting our mental evolution, and still others are sublime - expressions of our fundamental spiritual yearning. If we can gain control of these propensities, we can gain control of our minds.

Think for a moment of the process of colour photography. Three colours - blue, red, and green - are mixed together in various intensities, and the combination of these three colours gives rise to the millions of colours that make up the incredible richness of the visible spectrum that we see when we look at a photograph, or a painting, or simply open our eyes to the world around us. The human mind has not three but fifty psychic colours or propensities, each of which can be expressed at many levels of intensity. One or more of these mental propensities is always active to some degree in every individual. The combination of propensities that are active at any one time generates a variety of thoughts and feelings. When all the propensities become completely still, pure consciousness shines in its original, unaltered state and the meditator enters the blissful state of trance known as 'samadhi.'

Sanskrit - the language of mantras

As the investigations of the ancient yogis took them deeper into the subtle realms of the mind, inevitably they were confronted with sound and its meaning, the domain of language which lies at the very root of the human thought processes. Not only did they discover that language is the prime determinant of how we perceive the world, but they also found that each of the fifty vrttis which are controlled by the different cakras had a corresponding sound.

These fifty sounds make up the fifty letters of the Sanskrit alphabet. It is because of this intimate link with the human psyche that Sanskrit is ideally suited for the creation of mantras for meditation and spiritual practice.

Some years ago one of my students told me of a strange experience - he said that when he sat for meditation he did not need to repeat the mantra because he felt that he was hearing it coming from deep within his own mind.

The yogis who went deep into the science of mantra realized that this was the most powerful tool available for people to achieve spiritual liberation. Some of our fifty mental propensities are deeply introversial. The sound of the mantra awakens these - the purest and most uplifting of our innermost feelings; thus the mantra guides us towards infinite consciousness.

"There's a song I'm told that has no music,
And an ocean without waves,
There's a peace that passeth all understanding,
And I long to find it so."

From the song *Shanti*
by the author

2. Breathing

The next characteristic of a mantra is that it is rhythmic. What this means on the practical level is that it aligns itself with our breathing. Hence all mantras for personal meditation consist of two syllables.

Our breathing exerts a great influence over our thinking. The more rapid and irregular our breathing , the more difficult it becomes for us to concentrate or think deeply. When our breathing slows down, our capacity to think deeply increases. Take a person who has just been running for some distance and is breathing very heavily. If you ask them a question that requires some concentration, they will probably say, "Hang on a minute while I catch my breath." Conversely, whenever you are deeply concentrating on any subject, you will notice that your breathing is very slow and regular.

The alignment of the mantra with our breathing has two principle benefits: first of all, it helps to naturally regulate and slow our breathing, which in turn deepens our concentration. Secondly, an association develops between our breathing and the repetition of the mantra, which helps us to remember the mantra. When people become adept in the practice of mantra, they start to find that the mantra continues with their breath even when they are not formally meditating. Their minds remain in a meditative state even while they go about their daily activities. When they sit for meditation, they find it easy to remain concentrated, because the mantra is rising and falling with their breath. .

Now that we have some theoretical understanding of why mantras are so effective as tools for meditation, let us look at how the daily practice of meditation affects our day-to-day thinking.

3. The meaning of the mantra

"Without ideational concept, the repetition of a mantra is a waste of time."

Shrii Shrii Anandamurti

The power of thinking - your mental object

Thinking, as we normally understand it, is an activity which involves a subject and an object. We can take it one step further, however, and distinguish between our mental object, the image we have in our mind of something external to us, and the object itself (bear in mind that concepts such as fame or good health are also mental objects). The thing our mental object refers to (that new car, your name in all the fashionable magazines) may not exist yet in reality. It may never exist. But the thought exists, and thoughts are, after all, significant events involving movements of powerful energy. When the human mind, the mind which has invented and which controls nuclear weapons and space shuttles, thinks something, it is a tangible expression of the most powerful machine in the universe.

I once read about a small group of semi-autistic children who were suffering from arrested development. They had not been able to make the essential transition from crawling to walking, and although there was no physical reason why they could not walk, their teachers were unable to get them to take the necessary mental step. Then one of the teachers had an idea. He taught them a new game. He tied a rope between two heavy chairs, and got the children to stand, holding the rope for support. They could stand when supported. Then he taught them to start taking steps supported by the rope, and they played at this until they could traverse the entire length of the rope. Each day he substituted a thinner rope, then string and finally cotton, so that without realising it they were not being supported at all and were walking. Finally he cut the cotton into pieces so that they could walk around holding the pieces of cotton. They could do it because they thought they could.

> "If you think you'll succeed, you'll succeed. If you think you will fail, you will fail. Either way, you are right."
>
> Paramahansa Yogananda

According to yoga psychology, mental objects tend to get expressed in the external world. What we think about tends to happen.

This idea is not unique to yoga. Nor is it a new discovery.

Tribal magic is based on the same principle - hunting parties engaged in rituals enacted a successful hunt before embarking on the actual hunt. The shaman would paint images of the prey being killed on the cave walls in the belief that if they visualized a kill, it would become real.

There is an echo of these techniques in modern sports training where coaches exhort their champions to repeatedly visualize themselves winning, jumping higher, hitting harder, running faster. Nowadays there are few people who will deny the significant effects on our lives of a positive self-image and a positive mental attitude, or the crippling effects of negative thinking. By thinking we are happy, healthy and successful, we tend to become happy, healthy and successful. The reverse is just as true.

The power of positive thinking

Writer Norman Vincent Peale popularized the importance of positive thinking early last century. It has become the basis of much motivational and psychological training in business and related fields, utilising a principle that has been employed in yoga for thousands of years.

Since our thoughts tend to get materialised, our negative ideas can also prevent us getting what we want. Our desires can fail to achieve their external expression for many reasons, but perhaps the most common is that the negative side of our imagination gets in the way, sabotaging our efforts. Our imagination has tremendous power and when this power combines with fear or other negative sentiments - doubt, anxiety, worry, insecurity, anger, resentment - it can nullify all the positive expressions of the will. It is like driving with the handbrake on. Part of us pushes forward while another part restrains us, and the result is a trip to the mechanic.

Meditation teaches us a style of thinking that synchronises our imagination and our will. We create a positive wave (or mental object) in our mind and then make efforts to focus our attention on it. Whenever negative thought patterns arise and threaten to pull us in a different direction, we redirect our mind back to that positive wave, thereby training ourselves to overcome the distracting or inhibiting influence of the negative thoughts. Through regular practice this style of thinking becomes a habit and starts reflecting in other areas of our lives, hence the common experience of regular meditators that their desires get quickly and easily materialized in the external world. However, this is not always a positive experience. Often what we desire is not what is best for our growth, and meditators soon learn that they must exercise control over their desires for the simple reason that they so often come true.

The scriptures are full of stories of people who learnt the hard way that getting what you want is not always a good thing. Remember King Midas who, in his greed, wished that all that he touched would turn to gold. For a time he enjoyed his newfound wealth, but then his own daughter, returning from a journey, rushed to embrace him before he could stop her, and she turned to into a golden statue.

> *"The only thing worse than not getting what you want, is getting what you want."*
>
> Oscar Wilde

While meditation practice has much in common with the various schools of positive thinking, there are several crucial differences. Rather than utilising numerous mental objects (for example, different affirmations) and thereby diffusing our focus, we meditate on one object, which enables us to harness the full power of the mind. And that object is the subtlest object available, consciousness itself; it therefore leads us to the greatest possible growth and expansion of mind. There is an inherent limitation in a programme of positive thinking, if the objective is simply to develop a strong, positive self-image and a sense of well being. We may get all that, we may even become rich or influential, if that is what we really want, but there is no guarantee that even this will bring us lasting happiness.

> *"People are generally about as happy as they decide to be."*
>
> Abraham Lincoln

Mental power

You were thinking of someone when the phone rang and guess who was on the other end of the phone? You want to go to a concert but can't get a seat; suddenly a friend tells you she has an extra ticket for the show and wonders if you would like it. Has anything like this ever happened to you? Were these coincidences or were they small examples of the powerful connection between thought and physical reality? Meditators everywhere notice a startling increase in the number of such 'coincidences' in their lives after they start meditating. Whether it so happens that meditation speeds up the process by which thoughts are translated into physical reality, or whether it just makes us more aware of our thoughts and how they shape our lives, this phenomenon points directly to the tendency of our mental objects to find expression in the external world.

Let us examine more closely how a thought finds expression in the external world. Suppose a desire arises in your mind. That desire activates your imagination. Your mind paints a picture for you of the desired object and, consciously or unconsciously, you visualize yourself achieving it. Spurred on by the power of that thought-wave, you apply your will power and determination to the materialization of your desire. This is the driving force - desire, imagination and will power - which enables you to translate a thought into reality, though often most or all of this process is unconscious, and you are only aware of your sense of surprise when you find your desire materialised.

But the opposite can also be true. There are many examples of individuals who developed psychic powers through the practice of concentration techniques, but who eventually degenerated due to that same practice because they became deluded or allowed their minds to focus on selfish desires. In his youth the yogi Milarepa developed great mental power and used it to avenge wrong done to his family. He later realized how he had allowed himself to degenerate and after undergoing severe spiritual trials became one of Tibet's greatest yogis. That is why yogis always warn of the dangers of directing the mind towards crude or selfish objectives. Looking at it from this perspective underscores once again the importance of what we meditate on.

Beyond positive thinking

"The mind takes the shape of its object."

This old adage of yoga psychology is at the heart of the phenomenon of positive thinking. When you pour water into a container, it will take the shape of the container. Our mind stuff, that most subtle of all substances, acts in a similar way. If you think of a camel, a portion of your mind takes the shape of a camel, which is another way of saying that the mind forms an image of a camel. Now as we learned earlier, each and every expression of the universe is vibrational in nature. A thought is a mental wave composed of psychic energy or mind-stuff. Because it is vibrational in nature, that mental wave has a particular wavelength. The wavelength of the thought-image of a camel will not be the same as the wavelength of the thought of a vast ocean or a feeling of compassion. Some thoughts are subtle in character and some are less so. Subtle or expansive thoughts, as you might suspect, have a long, steady wavelength while crude or mundane thoughts have a much shorter, erratic wavelength. Our mind as a whole has its own characteristic wavelength, which is the composite of all the waves active in the mind at any one time. While our mind's wavelength is constantly changing as different thought-waves rise and fall in our mental ocean, it never changes radically because we each have our own habitual style of thinking - our personality, which determines the nature of the recurring individual thought waves.

Now what happens when two waves interact? There is clash between the two waves and each is to some extent influenced by the other. The stronger the wave, the greater the influence it exerts and the less it is affected by the other wave. When two waves are similar in character, there is very little clash. They vibrate sympathetically. On the practical level we experience this as a natural affinity or dislike for the people and things we come into contact with. Our feeling of like or dislike depends on the degree of sympathetic vibrations between our mental wavelength and that of the object we come in contact with. 'Good vibes' is exactly that, the good vibrations that come when we experience a parallelism between the wavelength of our mind and that of the person or object or environment we are in contact with.

Exercise - what do you really want?

"As you think so you become."

Yoga proverb

Before you read this next section, please get out a pen and paper.

Got them? OK, Now write down the answer to each question below before you read the next question.

If the mind truly takes on the shape of its object, and we tend to become what we think, we should be careful what we think about. Meditation is not just ordinary thinking - it is concentrated thinking; it amplifies the effect of our thoughts. And when you consider how much time we spend in meditation thinking about one thing, this concept takes on an even greater significance.

1. If you meditate for one hour a day for the rest of your life, how long is that in total?

Of course no one knows how long they are going to live. But for every ten more years you live, you'll be spending 3650 hours concentrating on one idea in a universe where thoughts tend to become real.

2. So what are you going to think about? Whatever it is, you are probably going to get it, so choose carefully. What do you want more than anything else in the whole world?

Write it down. Put down this book, and write down what you want more than anything in the whole world.

3. Now if, on reflection, your answer seems inadequate, ask yourself this. Why do I want this? Is it in order to get something else? Or is it an end in itself? When you feel that you have identified the fundamental desire behind all of your other desires, turn the page.

64

Love

Peace

Happiness

I've asked this question to hundreds of groups. And I continue to be amazed by the answers. They are all the same. Everyone wants the same thing. Usually it is expressed in one of these three words.

4. One more question. How much of this love, peace or happiness do you want?

Let me guess: A little bit? Do you want it to stop - to run out? Are you going to miss feeling unhappy? Do you want your joy to come with an expiry date?

Or do you want the real thing - an eternity of endless bliss?

Endless love, peace and happiness. That's what everyone really wants. All the other things we convince ourselves are important, or run after or crave, we really see as a means to achieve this end state - a state of mind where we always feel perfect happiness, unlimited love, eternal peace. Is this beginning to sound familiar? Isn't this what the great spiritual teachers throughout history have been telling us all along is the ultimate destiny of every individual? Nirvana, Samadhi, Satori, Heavenly Bliss, Enlightenment, Ananda?

We should not imagine that all those esoteric spiritual teachings have nothing to do with our lives. Nothing could be further from the truth - the message is for us.

So use your thousands of allotted hours well. Use them to think about what you really want. This is the way to happiness.

The ideation of the mantra

For a mantra to be completely effective one must be fully aware of its meaning. Although the simple repetition of your mantra is helpful, the full benefit can only come if we understand its meaning: 'I am consciousness', or 'consciousness is all that exists'. All mantras for meditation have a similar meaning, one which allows us to hold the concept of pure consciousness or pure awareness in our minds as the object of our meditation. Along with this comes a feeling. For some of us consciousness is too abstract a concept to relate to. It has no clear meaning for us. It is usually easiest to think of it as an infinite ocean of love, peace or happiness, bliss or God - whatever is closest to our experience. As our meditation progresses, we find that it doesn't really make any difference. The ocean of consciousness is an ocean of bliss and love and peace. It is the divine within us. And the essence of the feeling that comes with that thought-wave is that we are dissolving into that ocean, becoming one with it. The waters of the Self are flooding the boundaries of our ego.

It is this feeling which draws us back again and again to our meditation. We feel as if we have come home, and our home is at the very core of our own being. Even a short glimpse of the light of consciousness shining within us is enough to convince us of its reality and to fill us with a yearning to complete our journey.

"It is misleading to think that you are a physical being having a spiritual experience. Rather take the view that you a spiritual being having a worldly experience."

Teilhard de Chardin

Chapter 5:

Ego and Intuition

"The Cosmos is a bedlam of noisy confusion. Everything in it is subjected to a constant bombardment by millions of conflicting electromagnetic and sound waves. Life protects itself from this turmoil by using sense organs, which are like narrow slits, letting in only a very limited range of frequencies. But some - times even these are too much, so there is the additional barrier of the nervous system, which filters the input and sorts it out into 'useful information' and 'irrelevant noise'.... We all have this ability to focus on certain stimuli and to ignore others. A good example is 'cocktail party concentration', which enables us to tune in to the sound of just one person's voice among so many all saying similar things....Living organisms select information from their surroundings, process it according to a programme (in this case one that will ensure the best possible chance of survival), and supply an output of order (which is in turn a source of raw materials and information for other life)."

from *Supernature*
by Lyall Watson

Accoring to both Western psychology and yoga psycholo- gy the mind is composed of several layers.* Both theorise that the outer layers of the mind are mainly responsible for our interactions with physical or external reality while the inner layers are primarily concerned with subtler internal reali- ties. Yoga psychology regards the physical body with its central

---

Most people are to some extent familiar with the modern Western analysis of the mind into three layers - conscious, subconscious and unconscious. Yoga psychology goes a step further and divides the mind into five layers; the first two roughly correspond to the conscious and subconscious minds of Western psychology. The remaining three layers are sections of the unconscious, or superconscious mind; they include what Jung referred to as the collective unconscious.

nervous system as the outermost layer of the mind. It is here that information related to our survival is processed and it is here also that much of our conditioning is stored or expressed. Patterns created by past experiences are imprinted in our nervous system; many of our responses to external stimuli are determined by the patterns encoded there.

The controller of our conscious physical actions is the ego. 'Ego' in Latin means 'I'; it is the ego, which we ordinarily think of as our 'self'. The western division of the mind into conscious, subconscious and personal unconscious essentially refers to the functions of the ego. The ego processes the information received by the senses and translates our thoughts into actions. Though human beings have instincts like all other living organisms, most of our activity is controlled and directed by the inner self. Without it we would all die; it is the source of our intelligence and it compels us to act in order to survive.

According to yoga psychology, the fundamental quality that sustains the ego is the sense of doer-ship. Ego is the feeling 'I am doing' or 'I am the doer'. It can make you feel so involved in an activity that you do not feel any clear distinction between your sense of 'I' and your action. 'I am going to the shop, I am eating, I feel happy, I feel sad.'

> "...it is primarily upon the activating capacity of the ego that the process of physical activity depends. It is also on this activating (radiating) capacity of a person that their personality depends. The more developed the radiating power, the more shining will be the personality."

> Shrii Shrii Anandamurti

Our ego-self has its limitations, as we shall soon see, but it also has its special gifts. Indeed it has an indispensable role to play in the life of a human being. Without the ego we could not function in the world. We need it to get to work in the morning and we need it to get home at night. Someone has to drive the car and pay attention to the traffic lights. With the ego's capacity for rational thinking, its flights of imagination and its determination and willpower, it is able to act in the world and bring its desires to fruition. The more clearly it thinks, the greater its imaginative powers and the stronger its will power, the more we are able to accomplish and the more control we will have over our lives. Behind every success story you will find a strong and developed ego. Just as we need to develop and strengthen our bodies through diet and exercise, we need to strengthen this ego which manages all the mundane aspects of our existence and enables us to achieve what we strive for in the world.

Meditation is not about neglecting our bodies or negating our ego-self. Rather, its purpose is to develop and strengthen all the layers of our mind. The stronger the various layers are, the easier it will be for us to cross the boundaries of the ego-self to reach the vastness of our Greater Self. Regular meditation strengthens our ego by building our capacity to control our mind and direct it towards a goal. As we develop this ability, we feel its effects in every area of our life. We are able to focus more clearly on our goals and to pursue them with increased determination and mental stamina. Experienced meditators all share the feeling that there is almost nothing they could not achieve if they were to put their minds to it.

But the ego does have its limitations, and we add to the problem by assuming that this ego is all there is to know about ourselves. The ego is only the visible portion of the iceberg of the Self, and to remain oblivious to the far greater submerged part is as dangerous for us as it was for the Titanic, when it made its ill-fated crossing of the Atlantic.

> *"To the egotist He says, 'you are but a little spark and yet you extol yourself so much. I own the whole universe, but I remain silent in the background.'"*
>
> Paramahansa Yogananda

Let us now take a look at how the ego can trap us.

Faulty programming

> *"Life is a bundle of misunderstandings."*
>
> Avt. Ananda Bharati Ac.

Our interpretation of what happens to us in our daily life is generally determined more by our perspective than by the actual events themselves. Physicists tell us that what is 'really' happening in the physical world is that a host of sub-atomic particles are flying around at incredible speeds in the middle of a great void, and these particles themselves are just wave forms or energy within the mysterious fabric of space-time. However, we don't see any of this, and our experience of reality varies greatly according to our mother tongue, our conceptual framework, our upbringing, our biases and our conditioning. They are the coloured spectacles through which we view this whirling dance of atomic particles.

If we are to understand anything or even to survive, we need these spectacles to protect our eyes and enable us to interpret what we see. Every day we are bombarded by thousands upon thousands of different experiences and impressions. To cope with them we need to make instantaneous decisions. Time is short, so we all build up a data bank of pre-judgments, which enable us to make an instantaneous response when we need to. These 'prejudices' are based on past experience and they are handed down to us by our family, friends and social institutions. They shape our personality and condition the way we react to our environment. But sometimes the programming goes wrong. There is a faulty input at one end and we misread reality.

Here's a story that Declan, a friend of mine, told me:

When I was living in New Zealand, a thirteen-year-old boy, Ramesh, came to live with me in our meditation centre in Auckland. Ramesh was part Maori and was very courageous and intelligent. One morning I was busy planning the day's activities with my colleagues and preparing some papers for an appointment I had later in the day. When it was time to leave I picked up the phone to make some urgent calls but Ramesh was on the line. I must have picked up the receiver a dozen times over the next few minutes but he was still on the line. His little brother was visiting and I was sure they were plotting something together.

"Will you youngsters get off the phone," I shouted. "I need to make a few calls before I go out!"

"Can't, this is important," Ramesh shouted back.

"What is it that's so important?" I demanded.

"Can't say," came the reply.

"Right, you guys are obviously up to some mischief again," I said impatiently. Finally I insisted that they hang up so I could make my

calls and leave. As I was driving down the road with the radio on, I began thinking angrily: "Young people are so selfish. You try your level best to help them out and what do you get? Nothing but trouble!"

Just then, my favourite song came on the radio, a winsome ballad by the Irish folk-singer, Mary Black. I felt my anger melting away as I listened to the captivating sound of her voice. I remembered telling Ramesh that it was my favourite song and now, because my mood had changed, I felt embarrassed about the way I had been thinking about him. He was, after all, only a kid. It was his business to be full of energy and up to mischief. The song ended and the disc jockey announced: "That was a special request for Declan from Ramesh." The boys had been calling the radio station to ask them to play a song for me!

In another instance of misunderstanding leading to unintentional ingratitude, I heard the following incident that is reported to have happened in Ireland.

A man was working in the post office sorting Christmas letters. A letter arrived addressed to Santa at the North Pole. He opened it and read:

Dear Santa,

I am a widow with a seven-year-old son. I am on a pension and can't afford to get him the gift he wants for Christmas. I need another twenty-five pounds. Please send it soon. I have every confidence in you, Santa.

Yours sincerely

Mrs. Mary Aherne
10a McDougal Grove,
MacBride
County Cork

The man was so moved by the letter that he organized a whip-round with a hat and collected fifteen pounds, which he mailed to the lady, from 'Santa'. A few weeks later he received another letter to Santa from the same lady:

Dear Santa,

I received your letter with the money inside. I am sorry to mention this, but that toy my little boy had his heart set on costs, as I mentioned, twenty-five pounds. Unfortunately, I only received fifteen pounds in your letter. But then you know how they are at the post office.

Yours sincerely,
Mrs. Mary Aherne

Gurdjieff once said that before someone can break out of a cage, they must first realise they are in the cage. To the extent that we identify with our conditioning, biases and preconceptions, they become the walls of a prison that we cannot see. We become stuck in ways of looking at and dealing with the world that often only bring misery to ourselves and others. Before we can break free, we must recognise the walls of that prison for what they are. Meditation aids this process. As we develop our conscious awareness of the preconceptions that distort our perspective, we also become capable of seeing what is important to us and what isn't. Then we can keep the best and discard the rest.

Off course

It seems that in modern society we are trying to live our lives back to front. We are encouraged to own things, to do more things we like in order to become happier. But, in fact, it works better the other way around. First you have to find out who you are. Then you will know what you need to do, and you will have a clearer idea of what you really want.

This back to front approach to happiness is imposed, whether through coercion or a system of incentives, on the whole of society by the wealthy and powerful. At the beginning of the Industrial Revolution in Europe and America, and still in the developing world today, people had to work long hours at physically demanding tasks. The living conditions of coal miners and factory workers was only slightly better than that of the mules working beside them. Their physical bodies could not take the pressure of such arduous labour, and as a result disease and mortality rates increased dramatically.

In the modern business world, people expend huge amounts

of mental energy in the race to get ahead and be successful. The huge demand for intense mental work in the achievement of the goals of modern business exhausts the mind and nervous system, resulting in many casualties. For every jet setter who succeeds in keeping up the pace, there are hundreds who fail. Through the ranks of slickly attired executives exuding false confidence creeps an epidemic of stress related illnesses, nervous breakdowns, alcoholism, broken families and broken dreams. For many of these people their lives have become a gilded cage; their egos yoked like bullocks to the grinding-wheels of the commerce. They struggle to cope, but the pressures of modern living leave them with no time to care for their emotional and spiritual needs. And here we're only discussing the condition of the 'lucky' elite of this modern system.

"Poor slave
They took the shackles from your body
And put the shackles on your mind."

Traditional song from the black
slave days in America

Our willpower, the drive within us to manifest our dreams in physical form, has enormous potential, and like our bodies, if it is used wisely, it can help us to progress in every aspect of our lives. However, when we overexert our will, things may start to fall apart. From being extremely dynamic, we may become profoundly lethargic.

I once met a highly qualified chartered accountant who had been managing an institution with a staff of more than 2000 people. He had been made redundant and due to his advancing age was unable to find a similar position to match his qualifications. This dynamic, charming and intelligent man suddenly felt listless and direction-less and had to force himself to keep active.

Our emotional life needs energy. Our spiritual life needs energy and radiating power. Your body can keep your spirit and mind firmly planted on the ground. Your willpower has the capacity to make the earth a heaven for you. But if your ego is tied to the yoke of modern materialistic society, your spirit will not go anywhere except to the bank, the shrink or the undertaker.

Modern life places too many demands on the ego, and our

entire being suffers for it. The ego, which controls the body and manifests our desires, receives more and more pressure to perform, to produce, to make things - things we can sit on, or drive in to the office, things we can eat or drink or wear. But like the body, the ego also grows tired from overwork. It can start to break down, and then frustration sets in. But even worse, we are told that our ego is all there is, and we believe it. So we think that there is no escape from the frustration. Society has left us to toil at the wheel because they told us that that is all there is to life.

> "...it is only since the end of the nineteenth century that modern psychology, with its inductive methods, has discovered the foundations of consciousness and proved empirically the exis - tence of a psyche outside consciousness. With this discovery the position of the ego, till then absolute, became relativised; that is to say, though it retains its quality as the centre of the field of consciousness, it is questionable whether it is the centre of the personality. It is part of the personality but not the whole of it."

> Carl Gustaf Jung

I did it

How often do we push ourselves to accomplish something only in order to impress other people? The emotional satisfaction we get from feeling we are 'somebody', in someone else's eyes, is often more important to us than the accomplishment itself. But when our self-respect depends on the opinions of others, it becomes a trap as hard to break out of as a steel cage.

> "Tell me how a person gets their respect and I will tell you who they are."

> Dale Carnegie

> "The intelligent man who is proud of his intelligence is like a condemned man who is proud of his large cell."

> Simone Weil

Of all the trips we go on, the one which has the least prospect of a happy ending is the 'ego trip'. Everybody tries to pretend, to put on a face, a mask, in order to impress everybody else, as if we were all participants in a masquerade ball. Yet the very people we are trying to impress are also busy trying to impress us. And in the end nobody is fooled; nobody is impressed, and we are left alone holding an empty mask on a stick.

We are unique and special, each of us, but our true uniqueness and beauty do not lie in the trappings of the ego. What is lasting and of greatest value in our lives lies beyond the conscious mind. This is the uniqueness that we all share but too few of us realise.

Beyond the conscious mind

"I am too old and too lazy to write poems.
Age seems to be my only loyal friend now.
In some life long ago I was (unfortunately) a poet.
Perhaps I was a painter (or some sort of painter) too.
As is customary, the world remembers me
For this or that movement of my hand.
My name is known because this hand moves thus.
But the real me, ah!
That they cannot reach."

Wang Wei

The ego is restricted to the realm of 'doing' and 'having', where 'having' is just another form of doing. People become trapped in this continuous feeling of doing and never realise that the greater part of themselves lies beyond the ego, beyond the feeling of 'doing' and 'having'.

"The purpose of meditation, paradoxically, is to learn to simply 'be'. Since nearly everything we do in life is done with some goal in mind, most of our actions are only the means to an end, pointing us continually toward a future that does not exist. But meditation, when no goal disturbs it, allows us to discover the richness and profundity of the present moment. We begin to realise the miraculous power of our own lives - not as they will

be, or as we might imagine they once were at some golden time in the past, but as they actually are. Meditation is one of the few things in life that is not about DOING but about BEING."

Rick Fields

Many people report that at some point in their lives, they have caught a glimpse of a pure sense of awareness, a sense of pure existence. It might have been during a quiet moment by the seashore or while listening to a beautiful piece of music. Such experiences come when our minds momentarily let go of our agendas and motives, our preoccupations and desires. When it happens, most of us don't really know how we got there, but for that one moment everything just 'is'and that 'is' seems perfect.

Some years ago I was staying on a spiritual community in India - a place called Ananda Nagar. I was walking alone one afternoon along a path through the fields, and I found myself filled by a sense of the most perfect peace imaginable. There seemed to be no need to ever worry about anything again. I desired nothing, I have never felt more content. This sublime feeling remained, to some degree, for several hours. I do not know why it came. I do not know why it went.

It is important to remember that this kind of experience should not be confused with 'enlightenment' or 'self-realisation.' Such experiences may be profound and meaningful, but they are just glimpses of the spiritual reality, and can as well occur at the beginning of the spiritual path, as near its end. So long as there is any feeling of ego at all, any sense of separation from Cosmic Consciousness, then we still have a distance to go.

The part of the mind that keeps us from enjoying that level of consciousness as our natural state is the ego. The constant movement of thought, the incessant coming and going, acts as a veil between us and this quiet, joyful awareness. If the veil is thick enough, if our identification with the ego is complete, we don't even realise that there is something more, a state of mind much more profound and much more satisfying than anything we have ever experienced. Then the ego becomes our prison, the bars between us and our experience of our inner Self.

There is a popular story from Japan about a man who was interested in Zen Buddhism. He had studied philosophy for some years and approached a famous Zen Master for instruction. He started telling the master all he knew about philosophy and what he understood to be the meaning of existence. After he had spoken for some time, he paused for breath. The master said, "Would you like a cup of tea?"

The aspirant was surprised, as he expected the master to respond to his erudite philosophical exposition with some words of wisdom. Out of politeness he replied, "Yes, thank you."

The master proceeded to prepare and pour the tea in silence, and the aspirant went on talking about how much he knew until he noticed that the master was continuing to pour the tea into his cup after it was full and overflowing. Then the hot tea spilled off the table onto his lap. He jumped up with an exclamation. "How can you be so careless! You are still pouring tea when there is no more room in the cup!"

The master smiled. "That is correct. There is no more room. Your cup is full."

"Discovery takes place, not when the mind is crowded with knowledge, but when knowledge is absent; only then is there stillness and space, and in this state understanding or discovery comes into being. Knowledge is undoubtedly useful at one level, but at another it is positively harmful."

Krishnamurti

In order to receive wisdom, we have to forget how much we think we know. We have to have what the Zen Buddhists call 'Beginner's Mind'. Before any more water can be added, we have to learn how to empty our cup. We have to learn to get past the things we do, the things we know, the beliefs we have, and go into the 'I' that is at the root of all these expressions of the ego.

The part of us which is beyond the realm of doing and owning exists in our pure sense of existence, in the feeling of 'I'. We all know the experience of 'I am doing the laundry'. What we miss is the part of us that is behind the doing. The 'I am doing' is forever changing. 'I am happy' turns into 'I am sad' and the 'I am sad' decides to get up off the couch and take out the laundry. But the 'I' that experiences these various conditions is constant. The same sense of existence lies hidden at the root of every one of the little actions that string themselves together to make up the continuum of our life. It is the one constant in our life.

This 'I' feeling is also the one constant amongst all of the Individuals, the one thing that we all share. Remember the many moons reflected in the cow's footprints? Our individual 'I' feelings are just miniature reflections of the Universal. Consciousness, or Paramatman - the Supreme Soul, or God.

Meditation teaches us how to get to that 'I' by training us to go beyond all the mental activity that keeps us away from it. We have all experienced being caught up in a situation or an emotion and suddenly, for one fleeting moment, we mentally stepped back, and watched ourselves as we might watch a fish floundering in a net. But the moment passes because we have not learned how to break the bonds of our identification with the doer of the action, our sense of ego. We can only break the bonds of that identification when we quieten the activities of the ego, when we enter a state of stillness where there is no place for the ego. The ego has a natural fear of its own dissolution. We are afraid that if we stop being so busy doing or having, we will stop being. But the truth is, in fact, the reverse. It is only when the ego bows out for a time, when we stop identifying with our actions, achievements and possessions, that we become fully aware of our own existence.

Descartes based his famous proof of existence on the statement "I think, therefore I am", and this concept lies at the heart of the Western view of life. But this is a limited view of ourselves which fails to acknowledge the presence of a deeper self behind the thinking. It is possible to realise through meditation that we are not our thoughts, that our true self is the unchanging awareness of existence located at the core of our being.

Intuition

"You must merge the 'I do' feeling with your existential 'I' feel - ing. This is how human beings establish themselves in the realm of intuition."

Shrii Shrii Anandamurti

Intuition is the name we give to those faculties of mind which lie beyond the domain of the ego, outside the realms of what we think of as the conscious and subconscious minds. When an insight or fragment of information trickles down from the level of pure transcendental awareness into our waking consciousness, we find ourselves confronted with knowledge and experiences that the rational mind cannot account for.

At the age of sixteen I dreamed that my best friend, who lived five hundred miles away, had a car accident on a particular road. I found out the next day that he had in fact had an accident on that very road.

Perhaps you have experienced knowing what someone was going to say just before they said it, or you and a friend have found you were both humming the same tune in your heads. Or you might have racked your brains trying to solve a difficult problem, only to find that the solution came to you in a sudden flash some time later.

These are all tiny instances of what we call intuition, sparks of knowledge that cannot logically be explained by our narrow, ego-bound view of the world. Mystics throughout history, from widely different cultures and backgrounds, report experiences of communion with a mysterious, limitless intelligence that pervades all of existence, an infinite awareness that we are all part of, whether or not we are conscious of it. Their accounts provide us with a record of the possibilities of human experience that cannot be ignored.

> *"...Whatever the place or period in which they have arisen, their aims, doctrines, and methods have been substantially the same. Their experiences, therefore, form a body of evidence, curiously consistent and often mutually explanatory, which must be taken into account before we can add up the sum of the energies and potentialities of the human spirit or reasonably speculate on its relation to the unknown world, which lies beyond the boundaries of the senses."*

> Evelyn Underhill

One of the experiences common to all of these explorers of inner space is that all of life is interconnected because all of life partakes of the same consciousness, which is, in fact, the substratum of existence. Consciousness is one, they insist, but we fail to experience this because we are blinded to the deeper experiences of existence by the veils of our ego. Yet, if we look around us, examples of the interconnectedness of life are everywhere. In Supernature, Lyall Watson describes a somewhat horrific experiment done in Russia in the 1960's:

They took newly born rabbits to the depths of the sea in a submarine and kept the mother ashore in a laboratory with electrodes implanted deep in her brain. At intervals, the rabbits in the submarine were killed one by one, and at the precise moment that each of her offspring died there were sharp electrical responses in the brain waves of the mother. There is no known physical way that a submerged submarine can communicate with anyone on land, and yet even rabbits seem to be able to make contact in a moment of crisis.

For years naturalists were unable to understand how birds flying in formation were suddenly able to change direction all together. After analysing many hours of film they couldn't find a single instance of one bird moving first. The birds all changed direction at exactly the same moment; no plausible explanation could be found of how they communicated their intentions to each other.

Cambridge scientist Dr Rupert Sheldrake writes in 'Seven Experiments that will Change the World' of a dog that was filmed coming to wait by the door in anticipation when its mistress decided to return home from the far side of the city at an unscheduled time. These experiments were repeated on numerous occasions, effectively proving the existence of some sort of extra-sensory communication between dogs and humans.

Numerous examples of this telepathic communication exist among other species. Human beings are no exception. But curiously such instances are far more common among indigenous peoples than in the modern west. It is also much more accepted among them as a natural part of daily life. This suggests that it is the dominating and overworked intellect and associated ego of western peoples that erects a barrier between them and the realm of the intuitive mind.

C. G. Jung is the western thinker most credited with having explored the subtler psychic realities and those mysterious areas of consciousness that lie beyond the ego. Among his many discoveries was the existence of what he called the 'collective unconscious', a vast, transpersonal storehouse of knowledge common to us all. He found that his patients, while drawing images from their dreams, were tapping into the past experience of all mankind to draw symbols from other times and other cultures, symbols that they could not have possibly have come across in their personal lives. He found these symbols to be ways of describing the deeper, transpersonal elements of our psychic existence in the language of the conscious mind.

> *"A symbol is a mythological sign that has one leg here and the other in infinity. It points to the transcendent."*
>
> C. G. Jung

How do we develop this intuition? How can we gain access to the vast reaches of the mind that lie concealed by the activities of the ego? The secret lies in our 'I' feeling, our pure sense of existence. The next time you find yourself caught up in a situation, try to step back for a moment and get in touch with the 'I' that is taking part in the drama. "I am so angry"; "I've got to finish this on time". Focus on the 'I' instead. Watch it as if you were a spectator and not an actor on the stage. It is not easy, but we all have the capacity to do it, once we can shift our attention away from the drama. The moment we think of our 'I' and make the effort to concentrate our attention there, we have begun to step back into mindfulness, our awareness of self. Our inner 'I' is there at the core of everything you do. We only have to pay attention to it, to start identifying with who we really are and not with all the doings and owning, the comings and goings of this relative world.

The problem comes when the ego butts in and demands our full attention. It has its place, that of a faithful servant ready to do the bidding of its master, consciousness, but it doesn't know its place. Like a spoiled child it insists on being the centre of attention. And just like a child we have to treat it firmly but lovingly. We have to teach it where and when and how to behave. That's where meditation comes in. Meditation is there to teach the ego how to behave and to help us to understand who we really are. When we sit down to meditate, the ego is still active. We have thoughts, desires, preoccupations. But during meditation we train our mind to concentrate on consciousness, on the pure awareness which is the source from which all these thoughts arise. As we redirect our mind inwards, we become aware of the thoughts that pull us away from our object of concentration. We see the mind in action, the complexes, the anxieties, the desires, and the mad rush of the ego towards its fulfilment in the physical world. But because we are meditating on consciousness we become more and more aware of ourselves as the spectator. The thoughts become the background and the still place at the centre becomes the foreground, the place from where we sit and watch. Gradually these thoughts subside like foam in the wake of a departing wave. The inexorable joy of that quiescent awareness pulls us deeper and deeper inside, until all we find is ocean, the ocean of 'I', the ocean of our deepest self. When we get up from meditation we retain that experience. Slowly we develop the habit of breaking our identification with our ego and contacting the deeper 'I', the unchanging 'I', which lies behind the turbulence of our daily life.

In meditation classes the students sometimes complain that meditation is too simple. There has got to be more to it, they say. They want more to think about, to visualise, to feel. It is too hard to try to think of only one thing. But that's actually the point, and the beauty of it. It is simple and hard at the same time. Thinking and visualising are familiar functions of the mind. We use them as springboards in the process of our meditation; but eventually we have to leave them behind and venture into the unknown. We have to stop thinking and start being. Meditation gives the mind the bare minimum of ideas to focus on as a stepping-stone to the state of pure awareness.

"I said to my soul, be still,
and let the dark come upon you
Which shall be the darkness of God.
As, in a theatre,
The lights are extinguished,
for the scene to be changed
With a hollow rumble of wings,
with a movement of darkness on darkness,
And we know that the hills and the trees,
the distant panorama
and the bold imposing façade
are all being rolled away –
I said to my soul, be still,
and wait without hope
For hope would be hope of the wrong thing;
wait without love
For love would be love of the wrong thing
there is yet faith
But the faith and the love and the hope
are all in the waiting.
Wait without thought
for you are not ready of thought;
So the darkness shall be the light,
and the stillness, the dancing."

T.S. Eliot

Chapter 6:

Karma

"I cannot believe that God plays dice with the Universe."

Albert Einstein.

The chances that this immeasurably vast and incredibly intricate universe should be created and maintained by accident have been likened to the chances of a gale blowing through a junk yard, scattering in the air thousands of scraps of metal, and assembling in its wake a jumbo jet. Not simply unlikely, but for all practical purposes impossible.

Humans have always suspected that there is a mysterious intelligence behind this creation. We are conscious beings in a world inconceivably more complex than anything we could ever create with the limited intelligence of our individual minds. A few lone individuals have cried out here and there that it is all a bad joke or an accident, but by and large the human race has never paid much attention to them. We may not agree on the answer to it all, but most of us sense a hidden mystery, beyond our comprehension. Who or what it is, we are not quite sure, but who would not like to find out?

> *"You have come with the tremor of winter*
> *Who are you? What is this beauty of yours?*
> *Covering the green fields with ice and snow*
> *Who are you? What is this beauty of yours?*
> *In the biting north wind*
> *On the leafless trees by the wayside*
> *You wrote an unknown message."*

Prabhat Samgiita, song no. 94
by P.R. Sarkar.

Despite our lingering feeling that the ultimate truth is a mystery that constantly escapes us, we know that it expresses itself in ways that we can see and feel due to its impact on our lives. There are universal laws that govern our existence, laws that we can't escape because they are woven into the very fabric that the universe is made of: the law of gravity that keeps our feet firmly anchored to the planet we walk on; the archetypal polarity that we see reflected in every facet of existence - night and day, birth and death, man and woman - what the Chinese refer to as Yin and Yang. One of the subtlest of these universal laws, but one that is far-reaching in its consequences, is the law of cause and effect, the law of Karma. It tells us that every action creates a reaction, and that hidden behind every action is a cause.

This eternal chain of action and reaction has been likened to a pile of dominoes. One domino tumbles, after being struck by the one behind it, and it in turn sends the one next to it tumbling. Along the way it is easy to lose sight of all the dominoes that have gone before, but they are important nonetheless, each playing its indispensable role in determining the outcome of the entire chain. In the world of human beings some of these dominoes are made of molecules and sub-atomic particles, while others are thought-waves. Together, this intricate dance of particles and waves makes up the bowl of quantum soup we call the universe. Sometimes a thought-domino bumps a molecule-domino; at other times it's the molecule-domino which bumps the thought-domino, but in both cases it is just one more bump in a vast chain of cause and effect.

Let us say we decide to make a chair. From the scientific perspective of modern physics, a chair is composed mainly of empty space and contains billions of tiny electrical charges and atomic and sub-atomic particles, all flying around in an orderly fashion. The same with the piece of wood it is made from. Now we come along and take that piece of wood and carve it and sand it and paint it. Then we stand back and admire our handiwork, glowing with satisfaction because we have created something new. But did we really? Did we create the molecules that compose that piece of wood? Did we create the flesh and blood in our hands, which enabled us to carry out our work?

Let us stop for a moment and try to peer down that long corridor of actions and reactions. What was it that caused us to perceive this gyrating kaleidoscope of molecules as a chair? Might it not be due to certain 'pre-judgments' arising from past experience and conditioning. Can we even be sure that the original thought, the desire to make the chair, was in fact an original thought? Could it also have a cause? Might it also not be a reaction to something else, a single domino tumbling in a sweep of dominoes? Might it not be that subconsciously we wanted to make the chair in order to impress the people around us or to prove something to our parents or to fulfil some long-hidden need, and that each of these previous desires or psychic reactions arose out of other conditions that led to them?

It is perhaps the findings of twentieth-century physics, more than anything else, that has engraved this understanding so indelibly in the modern mind. Quantum theory has demonstrated that all things appear to be connected, and suggests that our mere observation of a phenomenon changes the nature of that phenomenon. The antiquated notion of Newtonian physics that the world is composed of solid objects and empty space has long since been discarded, prompting the celebrated statement of the English Astronomer, Sir James Jeans, that 'the world looks more and more like a giant thought than a giant machine.'

> *"One leaf, fluttering,*
> *tells of autumn*
> *over all the country."*

> A Zen Forest:
> Sayings of the Masters

The intricacies of the law of cause and effect are too great to be easily understood, let alone the vast mystery from which it arises, so throughout history we have turned to men and women of wisdom for explanations - to science, philosophy, psychology and, most of all, to religion.

As ye sow, so shall ye reap

Religions have always concerned themselves with the ultimate mysteries of life. Priests and theologians have tried, with decreasing success, to retain this field as their private domain. Nevertheless, no exploration of the ultimate mysteries would be complete without an examination of the religious view of these matters.

Every scripture talks about a cosmic law governing the consequences of our actions, and all of us intuitively feel its existence without ever having attended a single lecture or having flicked through the pages of whatever thick, black book presides over the religion we were brought up with or accepted or rejected. Nearly everyone feels that something bad will result from harmful actions. It may not keep us from doing those 'bad' things, but the voice of our conscience creates the feeling that we are doing something wrong.

Different religions have used this teaching in various ways, sometimes as a caution against sin, sometimes going so far as to use it as a clever means of manipulation or exploitation. People being what they are, we naturally try to find a way to escape the negative consequences of our actions. In the past the priestly class who claimed the power of intercession, took advantage of this tendency. For a small donation, they would promise to fix things with the big guy upstairs who had the inside story on actions and reactions, and the power to quash pending cases. They further consolidated their position by preying on people's fear of the consequences of their actions. Ancient and medieval theological literature is replete with grim descriptions of the torments of the underworld, a picturesque but frightening way to draw people's attention to the law of karma. Nor are these medieval concepts confined to the past. A few years ago a colleague of mine was in a bus station in Minnesota. He was sitting next to a man who asked him what he did for a living. When he replied that he taught meditation, the man looked serious and said: "You'd better shape up son. Hell's going to be hot for you."

Few educated people still believe today that another human being can possess the power to intercede for them with the cosmic command post. Most people understand that no one, no matter how well-placed they may be or how much money we give them, can change the laws of the universe so that we can escape what is coming to us. For better or for worse we are stuck with the consequences of what we do.

Don't complain. It's God's will.

A second, common teaching of many religious schools and doctrines has been the passive acceptance of the law of karma: a kind of fatalism which leads people to believe that because everything is the will of God, they should not try to change the way things are. This kind of thinking was propagated during the Middle Ages in Europe to legitimatize the oppressive rule of the rich overlords and keep the European serfs in their place. Such thinking is still widespread in India today - people justify the suffering of the poor, arguing that it is a result of the sins of their past lives.

In fact this misinterpretation of the law of Karma is sometimes deliberate; it is not even logical. If it is God's will for someone to be poor, and you are in a position to help them, it could equally be God's will for you to exercise your God-given faculty of compassion and help them. Surely this is more likely than the alternative proposition that a supposedly loving God created this situation in order for you to demonstrate that you have a heart of stone.

If we ourselves are the ones who are suffering, perhaps we have the right to adopt a philosophical attitude and accept it as a consequence of our own past misdeeds. However, to assume the right to interpret the cause of someone else's suffering, and then use it as an excuse to neglect or oppress them, is hardly a humane attitude, let alone a spiritual one.

It may well be that everything is the will of God, but does that mean we should not get out of bed in the morning? Or breathe, or eat? Even the decision to do nothing is a decision like any other, and it carries with it a set of consequences, the same as if we had decided instead to go out and try to save the world, or to sit in meditation and make an effort to master our minds. No matter what we do or don't do, we cannot escape the chain of cause and effect. The mere fact that we are breathing and eating to keep our body alive means that we are consuming the earth's resources. We are involved in a chain of cause and effect that affects not only ourselves, but all the living beings on the planet. We may trust in the wisdom of a divine intelligence, but we should at the same time endeavour to make the best possible use of whatever intelligence and energy we have been given.

"Trust in Allah, but tie your camel."

Sufi proverb

The easy answers of traditional religion often fail to satisfy the thirst for understanding that many educated people feel today. We sense that the causes behind our difficulties and concerns lie buried in our own past, hidden behind a dark curtain. The desire to understand the forces that shape our individual destiny fuelled the great upsurge of psychological research that we witnessed in the twentieth century and opened the way for the huge influence it now exerts over the way we perceive our existence. Psychologists have, for some, become the new priesthood.

From the mind's eye

Psychologists will be the first to agree that everything in the world is subject to the law of action and reaction, but they may not encourage us to waste our time worrying about the workings of a divine intelligence when everything relating to karma that is important to us, is already present in our own minds. Too much is beyond our control; whether it is an earthquake, or Manchester United winning the FA cup, or China invading India, who can predict what will happen? Can we realistically expect to understand the workings of a universe which is beyond our powers of comprehension? An event here might have an effect on Mars, as the physicists say, but will we even be aware of it?

When we go to automatic teller machine at the bank to withdraw money, we plug into a central computer system which coordinates the resources of millions of accounts all over the country. The amount of information that passes through that computer system in one day is staggering, simply beyond our comprehension. But need we worry about it? All we really care about is the money we've come to withdraw. That's what concerns us.

That central computer system is like the universal intelligence which ultimately decides whether or not we get our $10 and a chance to spend another Saturday night at the movies. It's a vast operation, handling the daily transactions of millions of accounts, but fortunately all we have to concern ourselves with is our own individual account. We have our personal banking card and this gives us access to our own funds. As long as we have something in our account, we can get it out at any hour of the day or night.

In the same way, what concerns modern psychology most about the law of cause and effect is how our past actions and experiences have shaped our personality. Whatever your individual destiny at the present moment in time, whether you are an alcoholic, a perfect mother, a delinquent teenager, the Pope, or a raving lunatic, this has come about as a result of reactions to past actions and experiences stretching back as far as your early childhood, which have been stored in your mind. The mind houses the impressions of the events that have shaped our lives and these impressions have given rise to the reactions that have created your unique personal situation in the world today. The key to understanding who we are thus lies in understanding what impressions are stored in our minds, especially those which have become unconscious, just as the key to figuring out if you can get the $10 you want lies in punching in the pin number of your bank card and verifying that you have it in your account.

> *"What we are now is the result of whatever we have done or thought in the past; and whatever we shall be in the future will be the result of what we do or think now."*
>
> Swami Vivekananda

Yoga psychology

Thousands of years ago practitioners of meditation formulated the law of karma based on their observations of both the human mind and the external world. The law of karma says that for every action there is a reaction. Newton discovered this in relation to the laws governing the physical world back in the eighteenth century, but the law of karma applies the same idea to the realm of thought. Thoughts produce reactions, as surely and as consistently as a falling ball will bounce up again.

However these reactions to psychic actions are not always immediate. In most cases, the reactions are stored in the mind as impressions waiting for the right conditions for their release.

If you poke your finger in a rubber ball and pull it out again the ball will immediately spring back to its original shape. There is a reactive force within the material structure of the ball, which opposes your action and wants to regain its original state. But if you leave your finger in the ball, the conditions necessary for it to express that reaction will not be present. You will have to remove your finger before the ball can regain its original shape.

The mind functions in much the same way. Any psychic action, whether or not it is expressed in the material world, creates a distortion in our mind-stuff or ectoplasm. Our thoughts have momentum, as any kind of wave does, and this momentum leaves an impression in our mind, much as a wave in a shallow body of water leaves an impression on the sand at the bottom. As long as that impression is not released through a reaction, the impression will remain, conditioning our mind and how it expresses itself. The deeper the impression, the greater influence it will have over our mental makeup and the more forcefully it will express itself when it is finally released.

A key point to remember about karma is that it is not, strictly speaking, the action which creates the karma, but our mental reaction to it. It is not so much what happens or what we do, but what we think that matters, although, of course, our actions are a direct or indirect reflection of our thoughts. Two people may commit a nearly identical act of violence, but one person feels remorse even while committing that act and afterwards vows to himself never to do it again while the second person derives a cynical joy from his act. The severity of the reaction that the second person will have to undergo, will therefore be correspondingly stronger than that of the first person.

When I was seven years old I was an avid collector of plastic buttons. I even ascribed names and imaginary personalities to some of them. The larger buttons were particularly useful. By threading a loop of cotton through the holes, and alternately tensing and relaxing the tension of the cotton, you could cause the button to spin at great speed, producing a marvellous whirring sound. The larger the button, the better the sound. Now I had somehow acquired an enormous and elegant brown button which, when spun in this manner, emitted the best and loudest sound of all. However, once my elder brothers discovered the powers of this singularly superior button it became an object of lust in their eyes. So it came to pass that one afternoon when I was playing happily with my button, they took it from me, and would not give it back. Soon I was in tears.

93

This attracted the attention of our mother, who demanded to know what we were fighting about.

"They took my button," I wailed, indignant at this new instance of the weak being tyrannised by the strong. My brothers of course denied everything, including the legitimacy of my claim to ownership of the button.

To my horror, my mother, instead of supporting my cause and administering justice on behalf of her youngest, as a mother should, took my beautiful button and smashed it with a hammer declaring, "I'll teach you kids not to be so stupid as to fight over a button!" I was mortified. Rather than achieving instant illumination regarding the futility of materialism, I found my trust in parental justice sadly diminished.

A few years ago I reminded my then eighty-year old mother of this incident. She did not remember it. Not because her memory is failing - far from it. No, it was because the incident had little emotional impact on her - from her perspective it was just the boys fighting again - hardly something unusual. I'm sure my brothers remember it no more clearly than she. But I, shocked at the unfairness of my mothers 'solution' was scarred for life. Well perhaps I'm getting carried away, maybe not for life, but you can see how an apparently insignificant incident like this can make a deep impression on a vulnerable child.

At least my mother apologised, albeit 40 years late. And I did feel that her laughter was inappropriate to the gravity of the matter.

Through our lives, as a result of our emotional reaction to different situations, impressions like this are stored in our minds, These become potential reactions, known in yogic terminology as samskaras. Karma is the action, and the samskara is the stored reaction. Often the word 'karma' is mistakenly used in place of 'samskara'.

Our personality or ego-self is, according to yoga psychology, nothing more than the sum total of the impressions in our mind, the potential reactions waiting to gain expression. They are who we are, or at least who we think we are, to the extent that we are identified with our ego. Our view of the world, our prejudices and beliefs and character traits, our complexes and strengths have all been created by our past actions and thoughts. Thus our daily life is a complex interplay of our samskaras, which we usually experience as what happens to us due to impulses that propel us along in a relatively unconscious manner, and our free will which drives us to initiate new thoughts and new actions. Our accumulated samskaras influence our present actions and thoughts, which in turn create new samskaras as long as we remain identified with our ego. Even though we may be unconscious of it, this can become a vicious cycle, robbing us of our freedom of choice. Let us now take a look at how eastern and western psychology help us to liberate ourselves from the binding influence of our samskaras.

Making the unconscious conscious

Our samskaras are, by their very nature, unconscious until activated by a thought process or external stimulus. The reasons why we think and act in certain ways remain largely hidden to us until we actively seek them out. The majority of people today are, however, far too 'busy' to take the time to uncover the hidden motives behind their actions. They are so caught up in the dynamic flow of their lives that they often imagine themselves to be the sole controllers of their world, never realizing to what extent they are driven by the accumulated momentum of their past thoughts and actions.

When people do awaken to the fact that they are the passive sufferers of their past conditioning, or more commonly, when some heavy reaction occurs which causes them great suffering in their life, they begin to search for some means to liberate them-selves from their psychic burdens. Lying on the psychologist's couch, they unburden themselves of their problems, and the ther-apist guides them back down the corridors of memory to find what hidden traumas or experiences might lie at the source of the difficulties they are now experiencing. This can be a difficult and often painful process as the therapist and client endeavour to peel back the layers that lie between the client's conscious awareness and the stored impressions in his or her mind.

"Consciousness naturally resists anything unconscious and unknown... (we) erect psychological barriers to protect ourselves from the shock of facing anything new."

C.G. Jung

The latent force which is stored in an impression is often released by the simple process of bringing what was unconscious into consciousness. Simply becoming aware of the original cause of our present anxiety is often enough to loosen its hold over us. The memory will remain, but the emotional power that was locked in that memory, the hidden tension associated with it that had so profoundly influenced our thinking and emotional state without our being aware of it, disappears. We experience that energy as it is released; it may bring tears or pain, but once it is expressed, we feel free. It is as if we had freed a fire-breathing dragon that had made its home in some dark corner of our mind, and we are now no longer a victim of its scorching breath. We relive the emotions associated with that forgotten or suppressed experience and when we wake up the next day, we find that we are no longer afraid of snakes, or that our long unconscious resentment of our father has changed to a conscious understanding. It is important to remember, however, that becoming conscious does not only involve gaining an intellectual understanding of oneself. The emotional energy that was stored in that impression had to be experienced and released.

"In the intensity of the emotional disturbance itself lies the value, the energy which he should have at his disposal in order to remedy the state of reduced adaptation. Nothing is achieved by repressing this state or devaluing it rationally."

C.G Jung

An inescapable part of our personal development involves this journey into the dark forests of the mind to confront the demons and witches and dragons that are lying in wait there. To wage war against them and chase them away with the light of awareness means a victorious return to full consciousness. This is the beginning of psychological freedom, which is nothing more than the awareness and release of these potential reactions or samskaras. It can be a difficult and challenging journey, fraught with painful confrontations with our repressed desires, sorrows, and mental scars. But it brings with it the taste of freedom, the opportunity to become an increasingly conscious being whose choices are our own, not those of a person who is just blown about by the winds of their past karma.

As Jung has pointed out, there is nothing to be gained by avoiding our samskaras and everything to be lost. While this attitude of actively facing and working through our samskaras can lead to some difficult lessons, those difficulties are nothing more than growing pains on the road to freedom.

"Your pain is the breaking of the shell
that encloses your understanding.
Even as the stone of the fruit must break, that its heart may
stand in the sun, so must you know pain.
And could you keep your heart in wonder
at the daily miracles of your life,
your pain would not seem less wondrous than your joy;
And you would accept the seasons of your heart, even as you
have always accepted the seasons that pass over your fields."

Kahlil Gibran

The meditator's approach

Western psychology relies on an analyst to help us explore the stored impressions from the past that affect our life. The yogic approach is somewhat different. Although it shares some essential elements with Western psychology and encourages us to take guidance from a spiritual teacher, it does not propose that the teacher should take the role of an analyst. Rather it encourages us to develop our positive qualities and to employ self analysis.

A few years ago I spent a week alone in Switzerland, staying by a beautiful lake on a personal retreat. I did a lot of meditation, wrote music, and practised creative writing as a kind of self-analysis. At the end of the week I was on a train going to Germany, writing about my experience. As I wrote, my mind was suddenly flooded with profound realizations about my own personality, my childhood, my relationship with my mother, and how these all influence my relationships with other people even today. This experience continued for about two hours. Although it was quite intense, I felt completely calm and by the end of it I was so much at peace with myself that I couldn't understand how I had ever felt disturbed by anything in my life. It was a wonder-

ful experience; and certainly resolved some deeply buried samskaras of my own. It was strongly reminiscent of the realizations I
imagine you're supposed to achieve from a series of sessions with
a good psychoanalyst. Perhaps I should have sent myself a large
bill!

In addition to there being no second person acting as analyst,
there is another fundamental difference between meditation and
psychoanalysis, and that is the goal itself. Western psychology is
primarily concerned with releasing the unconscious elements of
our mind that prevent us from leading a happy and well-adjusted
life. It is not usually concerned with what lies beyond the mind or
the deepest aspects of the Self. (There are exceptions such as Brian
Weiss, who used psycho-analysis as a stepping stone to meditation and spiritual experience.)

But for most people on a spiritual path this is not enough.
They want it all. They want the jackpot - infinite happiness and
the realization of their deepest Self. But if the mind is not balanced, if the personality is full of unresolved complexes, if we are
driven by passions and addictions beyond our control, then
reaching that state of supreme fulfilment will remain as unlikely
as for the sun to rise in the west. The deeper states of meditation
will be forever out of our reach. Thus, on this point the two disci-
plines can be complementary. Meditators recognize the need to
free themselves from the samskaras that keep them from their
goal, and their meditation and associated practices become their
means to achieve that.

In meditation we do not focus directly on our problems;
rather we gradually become aware of all our thoughts as they
appear, while we try to focus our attention on the pure awareness
from which these thoughts arise, the inner 'I' which lies behind
all thoughts. Gradually we learn to be aware of the big picture,
the nature of our individual mind and watch the thoughts arising
from the well of samskaras. As we focus our mind on pure consciousness with the help of our mantra, we become aware of the
resistances and mental preoccupations that pull us away from our
object of concentration. The deeper we go, the more we become
concentrated on our inner awareness and the less we identify
with the activities of the mind; slowly we become a silent witness
to the mind. We recognize our issues as they reveal themselves
with the intense clarity of a concentrated mind. We become con-

scious of ourselves as an inner awareness, which transcends the turmoil and turbulence of our thoughts and desires. We find ourselves gradually drawn into the depths of an ocean of inner peace completely undisturbed by the waves which ruffle its surface. Dropping down into the silence of pure awareness, even if only for a moment, gives us the conviction that we will ultimately gain control over our restless minds and realize our identity with the tranquil Self within, and this inspires us to make greater and greater efforts.

Through meditation, this practice of conscious awareness, the impressions stored in our mind are expressed faster than through any other process, the more so the deeper we go. It is as if we were shining a light into a dark room in search of the passageway leading to the freedom of the great outdoors. In that process the contents of the entire room are illuminated. Even beginning meditators become aware of a speeding up of the process of releasing samskaras as their meditation progresses. There may be no special effort to gain control over a particular desire or addiction, yet in our daily life we find it fading away of its' own accord. Or we wake up one morning and we realize that a particular fear or problem in our life is no longer an issue. What has happened is that the emotional energy locked up in that particular samskara has been released naturally in the process of our daily meditation. Meditation is not always easy because the ego resists our efforts to uncover what is hidden, but with time it is forced to admit defeat.

I used to suffer from extreme shyness as a child, and though I gradually overcame it during adolescence, it persisted when I played music. For more than 12 years I had a strong phobia about anyone hearing me play the piano. But within a year or so of learning meditation this fear just dissolved. I didn't even notice its' absence, until I remembered what I used to be like.

Sometimes I notice people with a little tear in their eye when they meditate. After they finish their meditation they may not recall anything particular which made them cry, but are merely aware of the release of some emotional energy. Yogis call this process 'burning samskaras'.

At other times a strong samskara can manifest itself quite directly when it is burnt. A friend of mine had a young man in his meditation class who would be gripped by an inexplicable fear whenever he stood ten and a half metres above the ground. Yet he was otherwise unafraid of heights. At eight metres or at twelve he would remain calm and collected. Then one day in his meditation the source of his curious fear flashed in his mind. He had a memory of himself at four years old, dangling by one hand off a balcony ten and a half metres above the ground. He was smiling and calling to his mother. His mother screamed when she saw him hanging there and ran to pull him up to safety. He reported to the class that after recalling the incident his fear vanished.

Often the potential reaction expresses itself in the form of something which happens to us. We may get hit by a car while crossing Main Street or lose our job through no fault of our own or win the lottery on a ticket that a friend bought for us. We have to undergo our karma, good or bad, and that universal truth is reflected in the events of our life over which we seemingly have no control. Meditators invariably experience a speeding up of their external lives as potential reactions are uncovered and seek expression. A whole lot more starts happening to us both externally and internally. We go through major changes. The unexpected comes up more often than it ever did before. And on top of this, many samskaras get dissolved in our meditation before they express themselves externally. As a result we experience the reactions purely in our minds, which is where all reactions are ultimately experienced, whether or not anything happens to us externally. In the same way all the actions that create karma are really psychic actions, whether or not they get expressed on the material plane. Our lives become subtler as we are able to deal with our samskaras on the emotional and mental level without having to learn our lessons in the school of hard knocks as the less conscious individual must.

In today's competitive world many people still consider sitting quietly in meditation to be a fairly unproductive use of a half an hour, but they couldn't be further from the truth. Not only does meditation free us from the past impressions, complexes and conditioning that prevent us from being a happy, healthy, well-adjusted, fully functional human being, it also takes us on a journey beyond all of these into the supreme fulfilment of our innermost being.

"By 'activity', according to modern usage of the word, is usually meant an action, which brings about a change in an

*existing situation through an expenditure of energy. Thus a
man is considered active if he does business, studies medicine,
works on an endless conveyor belt, builds a table, or is engaged
in sports. All these activities have in common the fact that they
are directed towards an external, achievable goal. What is not
taken into account is the motivation for the activity. Take for
instance a man driven to incessant work by a sense of deep
insecurity and loneliness or another one driven by ambition or
greed for money. In all these cases the person is the slave of a
passion, and his activity is in reality a form of passivity because
he is driven: he is the sufferer, not the actor. On the other hand,
a man sitting quiet and contemplating, with no purpose or aim
except that of experiencing himself and his oneness with the
world, is considered to be 'passive', because he is not 'doing'
anything. In reality, this attitude of concentrated meditation is
the highest activity there is, an activity of the soul, which is
possible only under the condition of inner freedom and
independence."*

The Art of Loving
by Erich Fromm

Mindfulness

The more we meditate, the more this reflective awareness
that we enter into becomes second nature to us, not only while
we are meditating but also afterwards as we go about our daily
activities. Rather than completely identifying with our ego and
letting ourselves be simply carried away by the action or situation, we remain increasingly aware of our inner 'I', the pure consciousness that is behind all our actions. We begin to notice how
our mind acts and reacts in different situations. This quality of
conscious awareness of our thoughts and actions is known as
mindfulness.

By observing our mind, we become aware of the motivations
behind our actions, thoughts and feelings. We may find ourselves
in a situation which makes us angry, but rather than simply being
carried away by the feeling and losing our temper, we find ourselves watching our reactions as if we were watching a drama on
a stage. This reflective observation reveals to us negative patterns

in our mind, showing us how certain situations set off our anger like a trigger. We discover the causes behind the effects - a prejudice, a stored past hurt, a deeply imbedded fear. We mentally step back a little more, remember the tranquil consciousness that is our real self, and our anger dissolves almost as easily as it came.

Mindfulness teaches us compassion by showing us that we are ultimately responsible for both our actions and reactions. No one else can make us angry. Only we can do that. And only we can do that if we have the unexpressed samskara for it buried in our mind. Once that samskara is released, challenging situations no longer have the power to 'make' us angry. We may find ourselves at the receiving end of other people's inappropriate behaviour and even take steps to rectify it, but it won't disturb our mental tranquillity. Even if we see that someone is doing something wrong, we will feel compassion for them, because we will be able to see how they are driven by their samskaras just as we were formerly driven by ours.

Buddha used to travel with his monks from village to village, preaching the Dharma. He was extremely charismatic, a shining spiritual personality, and sometimes whole villages became converted due to His presence. In one village a young man, barely 13 years old, was so inspired he wanted to become a monk and leave his family to go with Buddha. His father, a farmer, was very angry and forbade him, but the boy ran away and joined Buddha's group. When the monks told Buddha He said, "Send him back to his family, he is too young." So they did.

But the boy ran away again, and followed Buddha's group, and again was sent back. He did this repeatedly until finally Buddha accepted him fondly saying, "How can we stop one who is so determined?"

One year later they returned to that village and the boy's father, the farmer, confronted Buddha, very angry. "You stole my boy away, you evil man. You are bewitching and corrupting our children and ruining lives. You black magician! Sorcerer! Child stealer!"

Buddha waited calmly for him to stop. Then He said, "If I offer you an apple, but you do not accept the apple, who has the apple?" The farmer was somewhat bewildered. He'd insulted this man and now he was talking about apples. He thought for a second. "I suppose you still have the apple, since I didn't accept it."

"That's right. Similarly, I do not accept these accusations and insults you have been so kind as to offer me, so they are yours." And He smiled at the man.

Good luck? Bad luck? Who knows?

An old farmer in China had a horse that he used to till his fields. One day the horse escaped. The old man's neighbours came by to sympathize with him over his misfortune, but all he had to say was: "Good luck? Bad luck? Who knows?"

The following week the horse returned with a herd of wild horses. This time his neighbours came by to congratulate him on his good fortune. Once again all he had to say was: "Good luck? Bad luck? Who knows?"

Not long afterwards, the farmer's son, while trying to tame one of the wild horses, fell off its back and broke his leg. The neighbours, of course, were convinced this was very bad luck indeed. Not the farmer, however. His reaction was the same as before. "Good luck? Bad luck? Who knows?"

War was declared in the country and some weeks later the army marched into the farmer's village to conscript every able-bodied young man. Because the farmer's son had a broken leg, they left him at home. Was it good luck or bad luck? Who knows?

As our meditation deepens and we develop our mindfulness, we discard our old concepts of what is good and bad and stop being upset when things don't turn out as we expected. We learn the wisdom of karma, that whatever happens to us is the result of our own actions, and we begin to build our future on the firm ground of a deeper awareness of existence. We lose our egocentric way of thinking and start to accept the ups and downs of our daily life as natural. By learning to play the game of life in accordance with the laws of nature, the laws of action and reaction, recognizing that every action we perform has an effect on the world outside us, we develop a sense of responsibility and act in a way that benefits not only ourselves but everyone around us. And we tune in more and more to the unchanging consciousness out of which all of experience arises, that blissful Self which transcends the world of actions and reactions.

*"While watching a puppet show, you feel delighted to see how
the puppets move their hands and feet, but you don't see the
person who manages the beautiful show by pulling the strings
from behind. Similarly, we notice the expressions of individual
minds and we come to know how one sings melodious
discourses, but we can't see the Entity who pulls the strings
from behind and runs the show. And the funniest thing about it
is this: the speaker, the singer, and the dancer all think that he
or she is the agent, the doer, and takes the entire credit for the
performance. That's why it has been said, 'One should be
humbler than the grass'."*

Shrii Shrii Anandamurti

Ultimately love for the infinite Self within breaks us free from
the chains of karma. We leave the last of our limitations behind us
and enter into an eternal peace that was ours but which we have
long forgotten. This is the end of a long road, and no matter how
difficult the journey may have been, we realize that it was worth
every step, when, for the first time, we open our eyes and see
things as they really are.

*"Train yourselves in the ideal of the lily, which blossoms in the
mud and has to keep itself engaged in the struggle for existence
day in and day out, parrying, bracing, and fighting through the
shocks of muddy water and forces of storms and squalls and
sundry other vicissitudes of fortune, and yet it does not forget
the moon above. It keeps its love for the moon constantly alive.
Prima facie however, it is but a most ordinary flower. There is
nothing extraordinary about it. Still this most ordinary little
flower is in a romantic tie with the great moon. It has kept all its
desires riveted on the moon. Similarly, maybe you are an
ordinary creature, maybe you have to pass your days in the ups
and downs of your worldly existence, still, go deep into the
feeling of that Infinite Love."*

Shrii Shrii Anandamurti

104

Chapter 7:

Open Your Eyes

"A human being is a part of the whole, called by us 'universe', a part limited in time and space. We experience ourselves, our thoughts and feelings, as something separated from the rest... a kind of optical delusion of our consciousness. This delusion is a kind of prison for us, restricting us to our personal desires and to affection for a few persons nearest to us. Our task must be to free ourselves from this prison by widening our circle of compassion to embrace all living creatures and the whole of nature in its beauty."

Albert Einstein

Once a spiritual teacher asked his student a question: "Why do you practise meditation?" "To become a better person," was the disciple's simple response.

This seems like a good reply to me and it gives rise to further questions: What qualities should we seek, to make us better people? Does meditation cultivate these qualities? What do we do when we open our eyes again - have we changed? Has our inner realisation given us some fresh insight regarding our place in the world? How can we become more ideal human beings, not just in thought, but in action?

Some people question the social value of meditation and mysticism, suggesting that they can become a form of self-indulgence or selfishness, seeking personal happiness, but neglecting others. With so much suffering in the world, it seems reasonable to wonder whether we should devote so much time to our personal development.

If we were to meditate, and offer no comfort to others in their suffering, sparing no moment for selfless deeds, our development would be incomplete. Spiritual meditation does not allow us to do this. It cultivates a sense of oneness with all things and compassion for others. This feeling arises, not because of some theoretical idea that everything is connected, or because someone told us we ought to feel this way, but because it is the natural expression of our true nature.

Indigenous people, who live in close harmony with their natural environment, often feel this connection more readily than city dwellers.

> *"Every part of the earth is sacred to my people. Every shining pine needle, every sandy shore, every mist in the dark woods, every meadow, every humming insect - all are holy in the memory and experience of my people."*

Chief Seattle*

This marvellous feeling of connection with all life, when we are in the midst of its embrace, feels perfectly natural. So why don't we feel this all the time? What prevents human beings from feeling love for everyone in the world, and constantly acting with selfless grace?

The answer this question we need to understand how the ego forms egocentric or sentimental attachments.

Sentimental attachment

If you ask a group of people what time it is, and they all consult their watches, often they'll all give slightly different answers. And if you ask them whose watch they think is right, you'll find that most people think their own watch is more likely to be right than someone else's. Why? Because it is theirs.

What about our cars? Our houses? Our clothes? Are these not somehow more important than those of our neighbours? We associate our 'I' feeling not only with our minds and bodies, but with all manner of objects that we have identified as 'ours'. We identify with people in the same way. If a teacher criticises your daughter, you will leap to her defence, but you are unlikely to behave this way if she was not your child. Your 'I' feeling is invested in your daughter.

---

* *This is an excerpt from the famous letter purportedly written by Chief Seattle of the Suquamish Indian tribe, in response to the American Governments offer to buy their tribal land. In fact Chief Seattle never learned English. The popular version of his message is an interpretation rather than a translation, beautifully penned by Professor Ted Perry.*

In Irish surrealist Flan O'Brien's comedy, *The Third Policeman*, one character has a theory about the remarkable relationship between policemen and bicycles. He maintains that whenever a policeman rides his bicycle, some bicycle molecules migrate to the policeman, and conversely, a number of policeman molecules merge with the bicycle, so that over time the bicycle becomes part policeman, and the policeman becomes part bicycle. If a policeman leans on a wall after the manner of a bicycle, it means he is already in serious danger of becoming more bicycle than policeman. And when bicycles mysteriously disappear from the place where they were left unattended, it is a clear indication that they are already part policeman.

This sure sounds surreal but isn't it almost exactly what we do all of the time? Some portion of our 'I' feeling to leak into the things we own, so that we feel that a particular watch is "my" watch. We can't bear to part with a favourite bedraggled item of clothing, or we develop an unnatural fondness for our beat up and unreliable old car, or a deep attachment to another person. And a little of the thing, or person, lodges in our minds, so that they in turn occupy a corner of our mental world, if the thing gets lost, we feel lost: if the person is hurt, we feel hurt. If we are not careful, the possessor becomes the possessed.

This is what is meant by 'sentimental attachment.'

Sentimental attachment is a very tricky phenomenon. On the one hand it is human and perfectly natural to feel more love for one's daughter than for someone else's daughter. On the other hand, this natural sentiment can very easily become exaggerated and distorted, so that we become over attached. We may become blind to our child's faults, or not allow her the freedom to become an independent adult.

Let us consider how these sentiments develop, and how they can in turn affect our personal relationships and society as a whole.

The evolution of sentiment

As a general rule, our 'I' feeling associates first with our own mind, then with our body, and then with the people, places and objects that surround us. Moreover, the level of sentimental attachment we have for the people, places and objects in our lives gradually diminishes in intensity as their physical or emotional distance from us increases.

Human beings are most attached to their own 'I' feeling. Our sense of 'I' ness defines who we are, and it is very difficult for us to see beyond this. People often confuse their body image with their self-image. They think that they are their body. They haven't yet fully realized that their mental/emotional self is different from their physical self.

Because of this strong identification with the physical body we identify more strongly with those objects or people in close physical proximity. We naturally feel closer to our family than we do to people living in a 'foreign' country.

This is what leads to the sentiment we feel for our tribe, our race, our country, our religion, our social class, or our species - it all depends on the degree to which our 'I' feeling has associated itself with them.

In a small town Norwegian newspaper a story about Mrs Klem's cat being stuck up a tree makes the front page. An earthquake in Bahawulpur killing one hundred people is reported on page 37, just next to this week's specials in the local supermarket.

Someone in New Zealand produces a hit movie. I feel so proud. Why? I didn't make the movie. It is completely irrational. That is the nature of sentiment.

Sentiment can be expressed in positive or negative ways. Identification with and pride in one's culture and language is an essential factor in the development of one's identity and self-esteem. But when it is expressed as hatred or disregard for another race, or class, or religion, or gender, or species, it can become destructive. Nationalist, racist and religious sentiments have given rise to many wars. Even in peace-time many people accept the current situation where millions endure avoidable poverty and suffering while a few live in luxury. Why? Because 'those people' are not from our race, our country, our tribe

War will not end, and exploitation and oppression will not cease, so long as narrow sentiments prevail, pitting one group against another in competition and conflict. Only when we transcend these mental barriers of division and hatred will we be able to create a society worthy of the name 'civilisation'.

Recently I was speaking at a conference on Human Ecology, Whilst acknowledging the valuable work of environmental organisations, I pointed out that the root cause of our environmental crisis lies within us as flaws in human psychology, as a lack of compassion and love for all living things. Another speaker had expressed frustration that when a decision needed to be taken to avert ecological disaster, there was a 'lack of political will'. Which simply means that the people with the decision making power did not care. At least not enough to act as well as talking. I told the group that so far as I can see, humans will only behave responsibly, with love and compassion for all life, when they undergo a change in consciousness. And meditation is a powerful tool to bring about that change.

At the end I was speaking with the chairman. He said, "I agree we need to get human beings to change their behaviour, either through spiritual practice, or through rational persuasion." He paused for a moment and then added, "the only problem is that rational persuasion doesn't seem to be working very well."

"When the power of love overcomes the love of power, then the world will know peace."

Jimi Hendrix

But a brief glance back through the tunnel of history shows that in just a few hundred years we have come a remarkable distance on the path of moral evolution.

In the 17th Century, if you'd told someone that slavery would soon be illegal, they'd have thought you were a dreamer.

In the 19th Century, if you'd predicted that within 100 years there would be universal suffrage, that in Europe child labour would be eradicated, there would be universal free health care and education, and that businesses would have to submit themselves to environmental impact studies, they'd have thought you were a utopian fantasiser.

In recent decades we've seen the collapse of political colonialism, the advent of the human rights movement, public demands for economic and social justice, the rise of environmentalism, and the unprecedented phenomenon of millions of individuals responding without hesitation to crises and disasters affecting strangers in far off lands.

We modern, educated humans are very different creatures from our ancestors. In many ways we really are more enlightened. Our minds have been expanded through education, travel, the media, and exposure to different cultures, making us aware of the importance of other lives, and of our mutual interdependence. Never before in history has there been such widespread concern about humanitarian & ecological issues.

We've made considerable progress in transcending racism, sexism, and the various other forms of egocentrism that reflect the psychological root causes of 'man's inhumanity to man'. Yet we still have far to go, and time is running out as we are faced by the greatest crisis our planet has ever known. It is now a matter of urgency that we take the next step in our spiritual evolution.

To evolve, we further we have to awaken our higher nature, and remove the bitter seeds of hatred, greed and envy from our hearts, I know of no more powerful method to achieve this than the practice of meditation.

Spiritual meditation culminates in the experience of oneness. In that state there is no sense of separation. Just as the sun's warmth touches every creature of the earth, so the love of an enlightened soul reaches out to embrace all, heeding no boundary.

Relative truth vs. absolute truth

Some Indian philosophers have argued that the physical world is not real - that it is an illusion, and therefore suffering is an illusion so there is no point in trying to do anything about it. Or that suffering is a result of people's bad actions or 'Karma', so attempts to help them will be futile - that they have to experience it themselves in order to be free from the negative samskaras.

But this argument is neither logical nor compassionate. Yoga philosophy proposes that although the physical creation is not the ultimate and eternal reality, it does exist in a relative sense, and from the point of view of its inhabitants, the world is all too real. If we have any moral sense, or human feelings, the suffering of others should matter to us, just as it matters to them. And although it may be true that someone is suffering due to their past mistakes, it is equally true that we are being given an opportunity to remove our own negative samskaras by helping them. If we have real spiritual feeling, we will not even pause to consider these points. We will feel that the infinite consciousness is appearing before us in the form of someone in pain, and will want to help them spontaneously.

"Past the beggar and the suffering walks he who asks, 'Why, oh God, do you not do something for these people?' To which God replied, 'I did do something - I made you.'"

Old Sufi saying

Someone once asked my spiritual master how you can measure a person's spiritual progress. He replied, "You can only measure this by the periphery of their love."

If God is Love, and spirituality is the endeavour to become more like God, the more genuinely spiritual we are, the greater and more universal will be our love.

Law of karma and service

"Neither fire nor wind, birth nor death can erase our good deeds."

Buddha

Often when we do something for another person, we imagine that we are helping someone less fortunate than ourselves, and that they are lucky to have us around. But in terms of karma, the opposite is true. We are in fact the main beneficiaries of our own selfless deeds. The irony is that if our primary motivation is to reap good samskaras for ourselves, rather than to relieve suffering, it will not have the desired effect. You may be able to fool yourself, or others, but it's a bit more difficult to pull a fast one on God.

"I slept and dreamt that life was joy. I awoke and saw that life was service. I acted, and behold, service was joy."

Rabindranath Tagore

Years ago one of my students came to me to tell me about a personal problem. It was not the first time he'd spoken to me about this, and I became a little exasperated. I said, "Why are you complaining? You're so lucky! You're a healthy, intelligent, highly qualified professional, earning heaps of money. You're good-looking, articulate, you have plenty of friends. Your main problem is that you are always thinking about your own problems. Why don't you go somewhere where people aren't as lucky as you and help them? Why don't you go to a poor country and use your medical skills to help people with real problems?"

It was a spontaneous reaction on my part and I didn't expect him to take me literally, but I was pleasantly surprised when a short time later he told me that he was going to India to work as a volunteer.

When he returned six months later I saw a remarkable change - he appeared much happier, and he told me, "Dada, after I got back, I realised that the main person I was helping all those months was myself."

"The best way to find yourself is to lose yourself in the service of others."

Mahatma Gandhi

"Love all, serve all"

This is actually the slogan of the Hard Rock Café - a purely commercial enterprise so far as I can tell. The first time I noticed it on a big neon sign the irony struck me. "Serve them what?" I thought. "Pizza and French fries?" Business is not service. Service means to give without expectation of anything in return. The term "service industry," seems to me to be a misnomer.

"Do something for somebody every day for which you do not get paid."

Albert Schweitzer

Most people feel the desire, and the need, to help others in some way. We usually express this towards our loved ones, our family, our friends, our pet rocks. But we are also members of a greater family. All the living beings of the earth are children of the Supreme Consciousness. At a deeper level we are all connected. If others are in need, it is a sign of spiritual awareness that we feel the desire to help them.

Service can take many forms. There is no need to limit it to giving to charity, or to our immediate neighbourhood. If we really want to help people we must find out what they need and try to address that. There's no point in helping an old lady across the road only to discover that she didn't want to cross in the first place. And there is no point in trying to convince people to practise meditation if they don't even have enough to eat.

There has been much debate in recent years about the effectiveness of aid work in developing nations.

Early efforts were adversely affected by a kind of post-colonial patronising attitude. Poor comprehension of local realities resulted in a string of expensive failures and the creation of long term dependencies. Tractors generously donated to villagers lay idle because of lack of spare parts or mechanical knowledge. Soil that had been farmed organically for centuries was depleted by the use of fertilisers or pesticides that the local people could not afford to buy. Rivalries, feuds and jealousies between different tribes were unintentionally fostered through lack of sensitivity and research. The list of mistakes and disasters clearly showed that it is all too easy, even with the best of intentions, to do more harm than good.

More recent aid and development efforts have proven much more successful. Nowadays more aid workers make a conscious effort to understand the local culture, and respect and consult the local leaders and the community, and include in their objectives the eventual goal of self-sufficiency.

But even this does not get to the root cause of poverty, which is often some kind of economic injustice.

Take the example of international trade. Trade rules today are skewed to such an extent that a cow in Europe receives more every day via government subsidies than does an individual belonging to the poorer half of the population in Africa. Poor countries share of world trade has dropped by almost half since 1981 and is now stands (just barely) at only 0.4 per cent. The United Nations estimates that if trade rules worked for poor countries they could reap benefits of up to US$ 700 billion a year - 14 times what developing countries receive in aid each year and 30 times the amount they pay in debt repayments.

In the long run, rather than giving direct charity to people in need, it is more effective to help them to become economically self-reliant. Here's the amazing story of how one man, starting with almost nothing, changed the economic circumstances of millions.

Twenty-five years ago Muhammad Yunus, founder of the Grameen Bank, was teaching economics at a university in Bangladesh. There was a terrible famine in the country. He found himself giving lectures on elegant economic theory and then walking past starving people on the way home. He began to speak to the local people to find out how they were living. He met an old woman who was making bamboo stools. She made only $0.02 per day, because she had no money to purchase materials, and the trader from whom she got the materials demanded that she sell them to him at his low price. The bamboo for a stool cost about twenty cents. At first Yunus thought of just giving her the twenty cents, but then he got a bigger idea. He and a student collected the names of forty-two people in the village in the same position. The total needed to make them all independent of the exploitation of the trader was $27! So he gave this amount to them as a loan, saying they could repay it when they were able. When he approached the local banks, asking for their support in expanding the project, they refused, arguing that these poor people were not credit worthy and that they would not repay the money. But they did, so he added another village and another. After constant refusals by the banks to cooperate, he started his own 'micro-credit' bank with the help of the government.

Today the Grameen Bank is working in more than 46,000 villages in Bangladesh. They have paid out more than $4.5 billion, in loans averaging less than $200. Their repayment rate is better than the commercial banks.

Muhammad Yunus, an economic theoretician by profession, didn't start this wonderful project with an elaborate theory or a plan. He simply saw a need and chose to act.

"Do all the good can, in all the ways you can, for all the people you can, for as long as you can."

John Wesley

How to save the universe

"We do not inherit the earth from our ancestors, we borrow it from our children."

Haida Indian saying

Long ago an old Wise Woman of the Cree Indian tribe, named 'Eyes of Fire', had a vision of the future. She foresaw the coming of the white men; she saw that they would make war on her people, and on the earth, felling the trees, slaughtering the animals, poisoning the air and the waters. But in the last part of her vision she saw that a group of people would come together, from different tribes, different races, different nations and religions, and that they would make the earth green again. She called them the 'Warriors of the Rainbow'.

It certainly looks as if we are now living through the period she foresaw. We read about it in the newspapers every day. More of the Brazilian rainforest being felled, famine in Africa caused by drought and war, the growing water crisis, global warming causing weather patterns to change… and most of these problems can be traced to human activity.

"As a carry-over from our animal past, we have a territorial instinct, and tribal instinct. We are an emotionally and spiritually and morally undeveloped species with a highly devel - oped intellect and resulting technology. As tribes at least we had some sort of balance. But we have lost touch with our tribal roots, but not yet developed a more advanced system to replace it. As you know, this has led to a state where we are in danger of destroying our own environment. Already we have destroyed countless other species, and wreaked devastation on huge areas of our planet. We have set up a system which is so unjust that the wealth of a single man could prevent the deaths of millions of children, yet it is not used for this."

Conrad Lorenz

Many people understand that humanity is heading towards self-destruction, but feel powerless to prevent it, so they go on living their lives, trying not to think about it, or salve their conscience with regular donations to charity.

But we can do much more, even as small individuals. And if enough of us do what we can, it will change the world.

I am not going to go into detail about the vast range of options we have if we want to make a difference. This is not supposed to be a book about changing the world.*

Yet in a way, it is. We are not islands. Every action we take, every thought that floats through our minds, every word we utter, creates waves that ripple outwards forever. An invisible power connects us all, and if we change ourselves, we will also change our world.

> *"This we know: the earth does not belong to man, man belongs to the earth. All things are connected like the blood that unites us all. Man did not weave the web of life, he is merely a strand in it. Whatever he does to the web, he does to himself."*

Chief Seattle

For if our world is to be changed, it will be changed by people. People like you and me. People who are moved by a growing feeling of universal love, and a restless urge to do everything in their power to save our beautiful planet.

> *"This is the true joy in life, being used for a purpose recognized by yourself as a mighty one."*

George Bernard Shaw

John Robbins, heir to the vast fortune of the Baskin-Robbins international ice-cream chain, made a critical choice some years ago. In the course of facing and overcoming a serious illness, he underwent a deep personal transformation. Emerging from his ordeal with a new resolve, he renounced his position in the company and his share of the family wealth and mounted a public campaign to make people aware of the devastating effects of the

---

* *If you want to read one of the best, I can recommend* After Capitalism *by Dada Maheshvarananda. (Available from www.eternalwave.com)*

meat industry in America. Through his classic book, *Diet for a New America,* and the Earthsave Foundation* that he started, he has educated millions of people and has greatly influenced their attitude to health and the environment.

There is no need to go to Africa or Bangladesh to serve our community. Sometimes small things can change people's lives. In the 1980's a woman in Sydney, Australia became concerned about the problem of loneliness amongst housewives in her community. Suburban houses in Australia are usually single story with a small, fenced backyard. She realised that all of the fences kept people isolated. So she went to all of her neighbours and proposed that they remove all the fences in their block so that they could easily meet and talk and their children could play together safely away from the street without anyone having to go out of the front door. She had to be very persuasive, but in the end everyone agreed, leading to a much happier, safer and closer community. One person can make a difference. There are thousands more examples like this of individuals who were not daunted by the forces opposing them, who were inspired by their vision of hope, and sowed the seeds of a brighter future.

The role of a spiritualist in the world

The rich spiritual tradition of yoga has profoundly influenced Indian culture since ancient times. This presents us with an apparent paradox. If yoga is so enlightening and practical, how is it that India is, in so many ways, such a poor example of what a spiritual society should be like? It is a land plagued by inter-religious conflict, economic injustices, human rights abuses, and casteism. It is hardly the shining Shangri La you might expect of the homeland of the glorious yoga tradition.

The sad truth is that in the arena of social justice, India has long since strayed from the yogic ideal of 'Dharma' symbolised by the wheel on her national flag. Although still clearly visible, India's high spiritual culture has been greatly undermined by the propagation of religious dogma, the divisive injustices of the caste

---

* *For more information about the organisation John Robbins founded, go to www.earthsave.org*

system, and by waves of invasion and occupation, most recently by the Mughals and the British.

In addition to this, Indian yogis have retreated into ashrams, or into the Himalayas to meditate, neglecting the society they were born into. This amounted to a kind of 'spiritual brain drain', where the very people who might have aroused more compassion, justice and enlightenment in their society chose to leave it all behind. This withdrawal is at variance with the original spirit of yoga which advocates a balanced life, and does not suggest that we have to leave society in order to search for spiritual peace. Rather, yoga emphasises the special duty of a spiritualist to set an example in society, and to help people to live more in accordance with spiritual values.

"All that is necessary for evil to triumph is for good people to do nothing."

Edmund Burke

I have a Norwegian friend who has spent the last 5 years in Ghana building water supplies for poor areas. The project now supplies fresh water to more than 4000 villagers, transforming their lives. The project is expanding and that number will soon quadruple. My friend lives in hard conditions - unimaginable for most Norwegians but he's told me that this is the happiest time of his life.

Another colleague of mine from Australia started a children's home in Mongolia ten years ago. She now cares for more than 100 abandoned children.

These people did not start out with a lot of money, or even special skills. But they were equipped with something far more valuable - a willingness to sacrifice their comfort and time for others. With this spirit, even one person can make an enormous difference.

I grew up during the cold war, and was involved in the peace movement from the age of five. Well, to be honest it was my parents who were involved, and I tagged along. But by the time I was twelve I'd more or less concluded that humanity was going to destroy the world through nuclear war, and I didn't see anything I could do about it. So I stopped reading newspapers and took little interest in world affairs. I found the daily reports of human folly too depressing and I felt powerless to stop it.

When I was 19 years old I realised that I wanted to be a yogi - I'd discovered something that gave my life a higher purpose - the spiritual path to self-perfection.

But I only felt my search complete when I found a philosophy that blended the oriental mysticism of yoga with the environmental and humanist philosophy of the west. I'd not only found personal meaning but my social conscience, (never really dead, only resting) had been re-awakened by new hope. Hope in the human spirit - in the innate goodness of human beings, and in the power of individuals to change the world.

> "We are not powerless specks of dust drifting around in the wind, blown by random destiny. We are, each of us, like beautiful snowflakes - unique, and born for a specific reason and purpose."

> Elizabeth Kubler-Ross

The beautiful revolution

> "Building anything on humanistic lines requires a foundation of real love for humanity. A truly benevolent society will never come into being under the leadership of those who are solely concerned with profit and loss. Where love is paramount, the question of personal loss and gain does not arise. The basic ingredient for building a healthy society is simply love."

> Shrii Shrii Anandamurti

There is kind of service that is not always appreciated but probably has the most far-reaching effects of all. If we can help others to realise their spiritual potential, to awaken their love for humanity, we will have roused a force that does not fade, but grows and multiplies, spreading good will and good deeds through immeasurable time.

Think about it. You or I alone can only do so much. But if we can foster in others the awareness that they are members of a universal family, and if sufficient numbers come to feel this in their hearts, we could create a veritable heaven on earth.

"You see things that are; and you ask, 'Why?' But I dream things that never were; and I ask, 'Why not?'"

George Bernard Shaw

I once taught meditation to a man who had been involved in radical politics all of his life, starting out in the communist party, and later migrating to the peace movement. He was a good-hearted man, eager to alleviate human suffering. He felt that it was important to address the causes of our problems - to find a long-term solution. Learning meditation was, for him, a considerable departure from his normal way of thinking. We became engrossed in a profound discussion, and I spoke to him of the Beautiful Revolution. The Beautiful Revolution envisages a society that promotes human welfare, enlightenment and lasting happiness: education systems redesigned to turn learning into a joy rather than a chore; culture restored to its proper place as an aesthetic and inspirational pursuit, rather than a mere avenue of commerce; our social, economic, and political institutions recast in a nobler role as means to ensure justice for all and instruments for the formation of an ecologically sustainable society based on humanitarian and spiritual values.

Our discussion ranged far and deep, as we considered what the world would be like if we could only treat one another as members of our own family. As we finally emerged from our beatific vision my new friend looked at me in amazement. I still remember the expression on his face. "Now that," he said, "is really revolutionary."

"The flame of a lamp lights up countless lamps. The touch of a great personality wakes up innumerable sleeping hearts. In the same way, the eternal glow of the boundless élan vital of Cosmic Consciousness has been illuminating the life-lamp of universal humanism since time immemorial, is illuminating it, and will do so in future even more intensely. That is why I say, the future of the human race is not dark, rather it is strikingly resplendent. So proceed on, ignoring the frown of darkness."

Shrii Shrii Anandamurti

Samgacchadvam

"Let us move together. Let us sing together. Let us come to know our minds together. Let us share, like sages of the past, that all people together may enjoy the universe. Unite our intentions, let our hearts be inseparable. Our minds are as one mind, as we, to truly know one another become one."

Rg Veda

Appendix A:

Next Steps on Your Journey

Learning to meditate

Where do you go from here? Well you have a few options. You could read some more books. You could attend a meditation class, or you could try practising meditation right away. I believe that to get the best results in meditation you need personal instruction, so my recommendation would be to find a teacher. However, if you aren't able to do that, here is something you can try until you can meet a teacher.

Introductory meditation technique using a universal mantra

In the Ananda Marga meditation system we generally use a personal mantra. However, there is a universal mantra which we teach as an introductory technique. The mantra consists of three Sanskrit words: Baba Nam Kevalam. Baba means 'beloved' and it refers to your deepest Self, the Infinite Consciousness or Supreme Consciousness. Nam means 'name,' and Kevalam means, 'only.' The literal meaning of the mantra is 'Only the name of the Beloved.' When repeating the mantra, try to feel that Infinite Consciousness is all that exists, and that its nature is perfectly loving and blissful and peaceful. Feel that there is nothing and no-one closer to you than that perfectly loving Entity. It is important to keep the idea of the mantra in your mind while you repeat the Sanskrit words. Take a look back at the chapter on Mantra to get a clearer idea of this.

The Baba Nam Kevalam mantra can be sung before you do silent meditation. You can sing it to any tune you like or you can use a tune on one of our recordings (check out my website www.eternalwave.com if you want to get a really nice recording of this kind of mantra music). After singing for some time, you should get ready for silent meditation. Sit comfortably with your back straight. It is best to sit cross-legged on the floor. Close your eyes and begin to repeat 'Baba Nam Kevalam' in your mind. As you repeat the Sanskrit words, also keep in mind the meaning. If your mind wanders to other thoughts, just bring it back to the mantra. Sit for 15 minutes. You can use a clock or watch to keep time; if you open your eyes before 15 minutes, then just close them and continue meditating. After some time your 'internal clock' will be able to tell you when it is time to stop meditating.

Do the meditation two times a day. In the morning after waking up and washing, sit for meditation. In the evening, just before the evening meal, sit for meditation again. If you can get into the daily routine of doing meditation you are on the way to success.

I must however emphasise that it is far better, and easier, to get into meditation if you have the encouragement and guidance of an experienced teacher, and can practice with a group. If you want to contact the nearest Ananda Marga meditation centre, go to www.anandamarga.org where you can find the addresses in your part of the world.

Please feel free to write to me at dada@eternalwave.com

Appendix B:

Practical Tips to Improve Your Meditation

1. Minimize interruptions

Switch off the bell on your phone, let your friends and family know that during this time you don't wish to be interrupted; close the door, close your eyes and for the time being leave the ordinary world behind. This has tremendous psychological impact. If, while meditating, one part of your mind is listening for the doorbell, or is ready to jump up if the phone rings, or to come out if someone wants to talk, it will be very difficult to concentrate. Give yourself completely to the task at hand, letting the people around you know that it is important to you. They will learn to respect it too. Establish right away that during that period of time you do not wish to be disturbed, making whatever arrangements are necessary (childcare trade-offs, phone message arrangements etc.) and you will feel freer and happier in your meditation.

2. Meditate at the same time of day

Experienced meditators find that if they always meditate at, say, 6am and 5:30 pm, when that time of day occurs they naturally want to meditate. Optimum times are usually considered sometime around sunrise and again sometime around sunset. The effect of the mantra on a deeper level carries over for about 12 hours, so if you meditate twice a day the subtle effect of the mantra can carry on all the time.

If one sincerely desires to explore meditation it is important to establish a habit of regular meditation. Twice daily, in the morning to tune in and charge up to start the day, and in the evening to establish a rhythm and harmony in our life. This twice a day meditation ties us in with the world's daily rhythms. It is important to maintain this regularity. People beginning meditation frequently report having difficulty finding the time to meditate. Writing out your daily schedule and then 'brain-storming' (figuring out possibilities and listing as many as you can) all sorts of different ways to make time may help to get over this hump. Experienced meditators frequently report a considerably reduced need for sleep (due to the deep state of physiological rest during meditation) and so may gain as much as 1-3 hours of usable time.

3. Twice a day, invariably

This is the key to success in meditation. If one sincerely desires to explore the heights and depths of meditation, it is important to establish a habit of never missing your practices. Meditation can be likened to a beautiful chain - each day we add delicate links; the overall effect is a strong and useful instrument. But if we miss a meditation we create a situation of a "missing link". In order to make the mind strong, try never to miss. Be uncompromising. Even in an emergency, it is possible to do your meditation for five to ten minutes if you resolve always to go it. Though difficult at first, in the long run it becomes like brushing one's teeth or eating something one just does without thinking.

4. Meditate in the same place

Try to arrange a corner or even a small room for your meditation place. Keep it clean and fresh and try to do your meditation there all the time. You will find that place becoming very meaningful for you. When you go to that spot your mind will naturally want to meditate. You can really feel this if you meditate in a place where a great yogi has practiced their meditation for many years. Of course you can meditate anywhere in an office or a car, on the bus, outside - but it helps, especially in the beginning to have a quiet and special place.

5. On a light stomach

After eating, the energies of the body are directed toward the digestive processes at the expense of the mental processes (we have all noticed the sluggishness that follows a heavy meal). Because meditation requires alertness, concentration, mental energy and 'awakeness,' it is helpful to meditate on an empty stomach. If you are really famished take a g lass of juice or milk or eat lightly. If your body is really hungry, your meditation may be distracted.

6. In a comfortable, erect posture

When meditation proceeds properly, there is a flow of energy upwards through the spinal column. Slumping or slouching impedes this energy flow, impairs breathing, and diminishes mental alertness. So it is important to sit as straight as possible. A firm surface is very helpful. Gentle stretches or warm-ups can help to prepare the body for meditation. Some people find that putting a small pillow underneath their seats alleviates pressure on the knees and induces better posture by elevating the spinal column.

It is important to be comfortable so that your mind is free to concentrate on the meditation process. If sitting on a rug, cushion or folded blanket is not comfortable, you may want to meditate sitting in a chair. With twice daily practice of good sitting posture and some stretches and warm-ups to loosen the muscles, most people are amazed to discover how relaxed and flexible their bodies can become in just a few weeks time.

7. Keep good company

One of the greatest supports through the ups and downs of your spiritual growth is time spent with others who are treading the path of meditation. Weekly group meditations are extremely important for the serious meditator.

Ananda Marga conferences and seminars offer meditators a chance to immerse themselves in their spiritual practices and learn more about the philosophy of yoga.

8. Read spiritually elevating books

The intellect, which has to keep quiet during meditation, also needs scope for growth and development. Therefore, it is recommended that one set aside some time each day for reading spiritually uplifting books. After meditation is a good time to take a few minutes for this, as the mind is clear and calm and more easily absorbs ideas. Take a look at my recommended reading list.

9. Talk to a meditation teacher

I am one of more than 1500 teachers who work with the Ananda Marga spiritual movement. Ananda Marga means 'The Path of Bliss,' and it is an association set up for the purpose of propagating the practices of meditation and yoga, and doing social service. You can find out more about it on the website www.anandamarga.org Our teachers are known as 'acharyas' which means 'one who teaches by example.' If you talk to an acharya you will be able to get answers to your questions about meditation and personal instruction, free of charge. Local members of Ananda Marga can tell you when acharyas are expected and what kind of activities are planned (lectures, group meditations, etc.) while they are visiting.

10. Persevere

People's experiences vary in the beginning of meditation. Some enjoy it right away. Others may experience a sense of discouragement or frustration if the results of their first few meditations do not measure up to their expectations or hopes. They may feel that it is their own fault, and even give up the practice with a sense of failure or inferiority. Everyone who has meditated has had to deal with this in some way. It is a great help to know that others may be also having similar experiences, and to understand what is actually taking place during this time. Especially in the beginning, the mind may seem uncontrolled. A great Yogi, Ramakrishna, once said: "The mind is like a drunken monkey stung by a scorpion." You may find when you sit down to meditate that many thoughts arise in your mind; you set your mantra going and then drift off to something else. Sounds and noises from without may sidetrack your internal concentration and your body may become restless. At times like this, one can easily get discouraged and think nothing is happening. However, many of the benefits of meditation come from deep within the mind and do not show themselves immediately. By constantly bringing your mind back to the mantra, you are building up your capacity to hold your mind steady in the future. If you have the determination to pass through any initial difficulties, I am sure that you will be richly rewarded.

Reprinted with permission of Ananda Marga Pracaraka Samgha.

Appendix C:

Astaunga Yoga - Eight Steps to Perfection

The goal of Tantra Yoga is complete happiness and the method for attaining it lies in the full development of mind and body and spirit. Animals develop naturally through the evolutionary process, but for self-aware human beings Tantra prescribes a well-defined method to accelerate our development. There are eight parts of this practice and since its goal is union (yoga) with the Cosmic Consciousness, it is also known as Astaunga Yoga, or Eight-Limbed Yoga.

The first two steps are Yama and Niyama, which are a set of ten ethical principles for human development. The idea here is that by controlling our behavior we can achieve a higher state of being. The idea is not simply to follow a rule for it's own sake. Rather the object is to attain perfection of the mind. When this state of perfect equilibrium is attained then there will be no question of 'rules' because the desire to do harm will no longer be present in the mind.

1. Yama - ethical guidelines

Ahimsa: Ahimsa means not to do harm to others in thought, word and actions. This principle is sometimes interpreted to mean complete non-violence, but in fact this is impossible to follow if taken literally. For example each time we breathe we inhale and kill microbes. In order to live, we have to eat something living. In this case, the spirit of Ahimsa it to we select organisms whose consciousness is least developed rather than killing highly developed creatures. Another question that arises is that of the right to self- defense. Ahimsa says that to defend oneself, or another, against an aggressor is justifiable. Even if you use force, your intention is to save and protect life, not to cause harm.

Satya: 'Action of mind and the use of speech in the spirit of welfare.' This means to tell the truth and act to promote the welfare of all. In cases where telling the literal truth will harm others, then Satya means we should say what is best for the welfare of others, whether or not it is the literal truth. Adherence to Satya brings about tremendous strength of mind and is extremely important for spiritual success.

Asteya: 'Non-stealing' - to not take others possessions, or even to contemplate the same. Those who want to steal but who refrain from doing so out of fear of being caught are 'mentally' stealing. Asteya means to refrain from both mental and physical stealing.

Brahmacarya: 'To remain attached to Brahma (the Cosmic Consciousness) by treating all beings and things as an expression of the Cosmic Consciousness.' The mind takes the shape of the object of our thought. If we perform all actions remembering that everything in this world is actually the Cosmic Consciousness in a transformed state, then the mind will move towards a state of oneness with the Cosmic Consciousness. In some books Brahmacarya has been described as sexual abstinence. This definition was put forward in the middle ages by priests who wanted to attain supremacy over ordinary family people.

Aparigraha: 'To not hoard wealth which is superfluous to our actual needs.' It means to live a simple life with only as much physical wealth as is actually necessary. It is an important principle in both individual and collective life, because if one person or one nation hoards wealth, it may result in shortage and misery for others. It helps spiritual practice, because it frees the mind of preoccupation with material objects.

2. Niyama - self-regulation

The first principle of Niyama is Shaoca - 'Purity of mind and body.' It includes cleanliness of one's external world such as the body, clothing and environment, as well as the internal world of the mind. Purity of thought can be attained by autosuggestion - substitution a good thought in place of a negative thought.

Santosa: 'To maintain a state of mental ease.' Desire creates a state of uneasiness. Upon satisfying that desire, the moment of relief we feel is called tosa in Sanskrit. Those people who are easily satisfied and remain contented are following Santosa.

Tapah: It means to undergo hardship on the path of personal and collective development. Acting in the spirit of service to others without expecting anything in return is Tapah. In the past some spiritual aspirants practiced self-inflicted hardships and austerities (like walking on fire) but such austerities do not provide benefits to the aspirant, to the society or to Cosmic Consciousness, so they are not helpful in spiritual advancement.

Svadhyaya: 'Having a clear understanding of a spiritual subject.' One should read and assimilate the meaning of great books and scriptures written by spiritually advanced people. Mere reading without understanding is not Svadhyaya. The importance of Svadhyaya is that it gives us contact with great personalities and inspires one to continue on the path of self-realization.

Iishvara Pranidhana: It means to make the Cosmic Consciousness the goal of our life. This is done through spiritual meditation.

3. Asanas - yoga postures

Asanas are postures comfortably held. This is the most well-known part of yoga, but their purpose is often misunderstood. Asanas are not the same as calisthenics or gymnastics. They regulate the functions of the body, affecting the endocrine glands, internal organs, joints, muscles, ligaments and nerves. Properly prescribed, they can be used in the prevention of many mental and physical diseases, and their regular practice slows the ageing process. They are intended to maintain flexibility and good health, and by balancing our hormonal secretions create a state of mental balance and calm, preparing the body for meditation.

4. Pranayama - control of vital energy

Pranayama is a well-known practice of yoga, but the principle upon which this practice is based is not widely understood.

Tantra defines life as the parallelism of physical and mental waves in proper coordination with vital energies. The vital energies are known as vayus or 'winds.' There are ten vayus in the human body which are responsible for the moving activities including respiration, circulation of the blood excretion of wastes, movement of limbs; etc. The controlling point of all these vayus is an organ known as pranendriya. (The pranendriya, like the cakras, is not an anatomical organ.) This pranendriya also has the function of linking the various sensory organs with a point in the brain. The pranendriya is located in the center of the chest and it pulsates in synchronization with the process of respiration. When there is a rapid pulsation of the breath and also of the pranendriya it is more difficult for the mind to link up with sensory perceptions. For example if you run a race of 1000 meters you cannot immediately eat something and recognise the flavor of what you have eaten due to the rapid breathing and disturbed functioning of the pranendriya. During rapid breathing it becomes more difficult to concentrate.

Advanced pranayama exercises involve a special breathing process in which the pulsation of the pranendriya becomes still and the mind becomes very calm. This helps meditation greatly. Pranayama also readjusts the balance of vital energy in the body. Advanced pranayama exercises, including alternate nostril breathing, and retaining the breath, can be dangerous if not taught with the guidance by a competent teacher. They should not be practiced by complete beginners.

5. Pratyahara - sense withdrawal

Withdrawing the mind from its attachment to external objects. This is an important step towards deep meditation. With regular meditation practice it can take us to a state of profound inner peace.

6. Dharana - concentration

In personalized meditation techniques, the practitioner is taught to concentrate on a particular point - this helps greatly in focusing the mind. There are also more advanced methods of dharana taught in Tantra which involve concentration on different points and colours. These techniques help the meditator to gain control over the mental propensities governed by the different cakras as well as increasing concentration.

7. Dhyana - spiritual meditation

There are different forms of dhyana. When Tantric teachers from India first brought this technique to China it became known as Chan, and when Chan was brought to Japan via Korea, it finally became known as Zen. Although there are important differences between contemporary Zen meditation and the dhyana as practiced by the Tantric masters in India, the root teaching was the same. Dhyana helps to perfect the most subtle layer of the mind and leads the person to the final step of Astaunga Yoga which is samadhi.

8. Samadhi - spiritual trance

Samadhi is not like the other seven steps in that it is not a particular method or practice, rather it is the result of practicing the other parts of Astaunga Yoga. It is the absorption of mind in the Supreme Consciousness. There are two principal forms of samadhi, nirvikalpa and savikalpa. Savikalpa is a trance of absorption with distortion or qualification. In savikalpa samadhi the person has the feeling that 'I am the Supreme Consciousness', but in nirvikalpa samadhi there is no longer a feeling of 'I'. The individual consciousness is totally merged in the Cosmic Consciousness.

Those who experience nirvikalpa samadhi are not able to explain or describe it because it occurs when the mind has ceased to function. The only way they can even know that they experienced this state is after the mind returns from this trance of absorption. Then they experience waves of extreme happiness and understand that they were in the state of nirvikalpa samadhi. The attainment of nirvikalpa samadhi comes after millions of years of evolution, and after prolonged spiritual effort. It is the final merger with the source of all being.

Adapted from The Wisdom of Yoga *by Acarya Vedaprajinananda Avadhuta ©1990 Ananda Marga Publications, all rights reserved.*

Appendix D:

Recommended Reading List

Here is a selection of my favourite books on meditation, mysticism and spirituality. Many of these are story books rather than being philosophical.

Available from www.anandamarga.org

Elementary Philosophy - Shrii Shrii Anandamurti
Beyond the Superconscious Mind - Didi Ananda Mitra

Available from www.eternalwave.com

Gem's Story - Yatindra
The Ashram - Devashiish Donald Acosta
After Capitalism - Dada Maheshvarananda

Generally available through mainstream distributors such as www.amazon.com

Autobiography of a Yogi - Paramahansa Yogananda
Siddhartha - Herman Hesse
God's Pauper (biography of St Francis of Assisi) - Nikos Kazanzakis
Tibet's Greatest Yogi Milarepa: A Biography from the Tibetan by Walter Yeeling Evans Wentz
The Little Prince - Antionne St Exupery
Cutting Through Spiritual Materialism - Chogyam Trungpa
No Boundary - Ken Wilbur
The Tao of Physics - Fritjov Capra
Zen Mind, Beginner's Mind - Shunryu Suzuki
Ramakrsna: Life of Ramakrsna - Christopher Isherwood
The Glass Bead Game - Herman Hesse (particularly the three stories at the end)

Web sites to check out:

www.anandamarga.org - Ananda Marga meditation and yoga society's official website. Here are more books on meditation and related topics, and you can find the addresses of meditation centres all over the world where you can learn a personal technique of meditation free of charge. In this book you will have seen that Shrii Shrii Anandamurti has been liberally quoted. His original works are available through this website.

www.eternalwave.com - my personal website where you can find out more about these ideas, and can also listen to some of my music!

Glossary of Sanskrit Terms

Atman: Individual soul or consciousness.

Cakra or Chakra: Controlling point of glands and vital energy of the body. There are seven major cakras along the spinal column. These are also the meeting points of the flow of vital energy flowing through the body.

Karma: Literally means 'action'. Often confused with 'Samskara'.

Kundalinii: latent spiritual potential of the individual. It normally resides dormant at the base of the spine until the time of spiritual awakening. It is often represented in the shape of a coiled snake.

Mantra: A word or group of words, that when repeated aloud, or mentally during meditation facilitate the awakening of spiritual awareness. The mantra is only really effective if the meaning is also kept in mind.

Paramatman: Supreme soul or consciousness in the role of witness of the universe, which is the creation of the Cosmic Mind.

Prana: Life force or vital energy called 'Chi' in Chinese, or 'Ki' in Japanese. The three main channels through which Prana flows run along the spine, one straight up the centre, and the other two starting behind each nostril and weaving their way back and forth across the spine, crossing at each the 5 lower chakras.

Samadhi: Trance of absorption of the individual mind into the Cosmic Mind.

Samskara: Potential reaction to experiences and one's own actions, stored in the mind. Often confused with 'Karma'.

Sanskrit: Ancient language of the Vedas, which is composed of the fifty sounds that correlate to the 50 vrttis of the human mind. Meditation mantras are usually in the Sanskrit language.

Vayu: Literally 'wind' - refers to the vital airs of the body that control life and govern many functions of the body including digestion, respiration and excretion. Balancing the function of the vayus is an essential element of Ayurvedic medicine.

Vrttis: Mental propensities. Desires, emotions, tendencies of the human mind are 50 in number, e.g. love, hatred, shame, anger fear, sorrow, hunger, spiritual longing.

Available from www.eternalwave.com

Books

**Close Your Eyes
& Open Your Mind
Dada Nabhaniilananda**
"Close Your Eyes" strips away the mystery to reveal how simple, straightforward and effective meditation really is. Whether you are a complete beginner or an accomplished practitioner, this book is sure to make you want to just sit down and close your eyes.

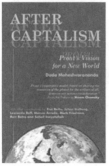

**After Capitalism
Dada Maheshvarananda**
This book offers a better, practical alternative to global capitalism. It explains the Progressive Utilization Theory, or Prout, a socio-economic model based on decentralized economic democracy, cooperative enterprise, the ethics of inclusion and universal spiritual values.

**The Ashram
Devashish**
Set in the picturesque hills of Topanga Canyon, within hailing distance of the glitter and hype of modern-day Los Angeles, The Ashram gives us a fictional look into southern California's colorful esoteric scene, where the forces of western commercialism and the mystical traditions of the east meld to form the beginnings of a new spiritual culture. Against this backdrop, we follow the journey of a young yogi in his search for enlightenment, from his childhood initiation by

a mysterious sage, to his fateful encounters with his internal demons and the suffering in the world around him, a stark reality which he must come to terms with before he can complete his inner journey.

Gem's Story
Joost Boekhoven
A heartwarming novel about the spiritual path and about believing in oneself. It is the story of two people in search of the Infinite. He is the perfect teacher, and she thinks she is his student. But who teaches whom?

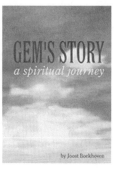

"The most powerful, uplifting, and spiritual book I have ever had the pleasure of reading!" - Dada

Music CDs

The Return of The Magic
Dada Nabhaniilananda
Dada recorded his newest album in five countries with a group of exceptional musicians. It has the smoothness of a late 90s' production with a 70's flavour - a kind of 'spiritual eco-folk'. Finely crafted songs, very groovy, beautiful lyrics, slick production. This is a powerful piece of musical magic.

Warriors of the Rainbow
Dada Nabhaniilananda
Produced by symphonic rock veteran Harry Williamson (who worked with Sting and played with British band Gong) this album has a grand style worthy of its theme. The music plays like a tapestry, ranging from sensitive ballads through a latin number to the reggae version of Give My Heart to Africa. Spell binding.

The Fire Dragon Suite
Dada Nabhaniilananda

By popular request Dada has released his
earliest songs on CD for the first time. Like
a secret childhood treasure being
re-discovered, this charming collection of
spiritual folk songs captures a mood of fresh
innocence and inspiration.

Eternal Waves
Sukhadeva

In his second album of chanting from this
Norwegian master guitarist has created a
dreamlike tapestry of intricately layered
guitar work and exquisitely arranged vocals
chanting samskrta mantras. His special tal-
ent is crafting melodies, and these are some
his best, creating a series of
delightful spiritual moods.

Flow of Love
Sukhadeva

Norwegian master guitarist Sukha Deva has
created a tasteful set of gentle, flowing
musical tapestries with modal chord patterns and haunting melodies. Overlaid with
beautiful vocals in a series of mantra chants,
this album is ideal for creating
an atmosphere for meditation.

About the Author

Dada Nabhaniilananda was born in New Zealand in 1955. He developed a keen interest in oriental mysticism during his university and musical studies, and learned meditation from a disciple of Shrii Shrii Anandamurti, the great Indian yogic master. He then studied the philosophy and practice of yoga in Australia, Nepal and India, where he met with the Master on a number of occasions. He has since been travelling as a monk and yogi, teaching meditation and performing music all over the globe. He has written numerous songs and produced several musical recordings. This is his first book.